1000 Strangers in My Car

1000 STRANGERS IN MY CAR

1000 Strangers in My Car

Adventures of a Pastor Turned Uber Driver

STEVE LA FARGE

CONTENTS

I'm Writing This Book So
My Head Won't Explode

I WAS A PASTOR FOR THIRTY-FIVE years. It was not what I planned to do with my life. In fact, the idea didn't even cross my mind until right after high school. But I heard about Bible college and was led to believe that it would be like church camp without the counselors, so I signed up for a year. God has a way of sneaking up on you, and while I was busy hosting all-dorm water fights and supergluing my across-the-hall neighbors' shoes to the ceiling, I felt a clear calling to the ministry.

I answered the call and began my career working with junior high and high school students, and for the final seventeen years, I was a senior pastor. I learned volumes of lessons along the way. One of those lessons was that there were things that could knock you out of the ministry.

I have observed too many of my ministry colleagues become ensnared in moral failures that blew up their churches and cost them their jobs. I have watched several of my coworkers get caught between warring factions in their congregations, and their ministries were chewed up in the process. A friend of mine made the mistake of introducing change too quickly until the only change the church would get behind was a change of leadership.

But I never considered that losing my voice would be the reason I would step down from the pulpit. As you might imagine, it's a bit more complicated than that.

In October of 2008 I was diagnosed with Parkinson's Disease. It should probably be renamed Michael J. Fox Disease, because he is the person most people think of today when they think of Parkinson's.

I had my suspicions before the diagnosis was delivered. My right pinky finger seemed to have a mind of its own. It would start to twitch, and I would try to make it stop. "Stop twitching," I commanded.

Sometimes it would obey, but it would usually ignore me and continue until it was ready to stop.

My wife, Barb, and I enjoy walking together. One time she was behind me and asked, "Why aren't you swinging your arm?" I looked down at my right arm, and it was just hanging there. I could make it swing, but it felt awkward. Were my arm and my pinky finger conspiring against me?

I eventually had to move my computer mouse to the left side of my keyboard because most of the time, my right hand would shake so much that I couldn't double-click on anything.

I finally got concerned enough that I had my family doctor refer me to a specialist. He was an excellent neurologist, but a little deficient in the bedside-manner department. When he finished his examination and told me I had Parkinson's, I had some obvious questions—"Am I going to die?" was the most pressing.

"No, Parkinson's won't kill you," he offered. "It will just make you miserable until something else does."

He explained that most people with Parkinson's die from some complication brought on by the disease, like pneumonia or cerebral hemorrhage. He rattled off several prescriptions that I would need to start taking to deal with the tremors. I could start to feel myself losing interest in the details of my inevitable mortality.

Then he said something I will never forget: "Parkinson's is a 'boutique disease.'"

That snapped me back to the present. I remember picturing a women's clothing store with unique dresses and one-of-a-kind handbags and custom jewelry. It sounded kind of nice. I have a "boutique" disease.

But as he continued, his explanation took on a more insidious tone. It turns out that Parkinson's can look and act differently on every person. It can basically do whatever it pleases to whatever part of your body it chooses. And my version had decided to settle, at least in part, in my voice.

When my doctor mentioned that Parkinson's can affect a person's voice, the alarm bells started going off in my head. Increasingly over the past year, I had been having trouble getting through a sermon or a lesson without ending up with a really scratchy throat. I had blamed the problem on allergies or just talking too much, but now I was sure that my voice was joining forces with my pinky finger in the conspiracy.

The problem with my voice got steadily worse, to the point that people were leaving the church because they couldn't hear me preach. The leadership of the congregation I was serving made a valiant effort to keep me at my post. They tried new sound equipment and expensive headphones for the hearing impaired. They even started taking over parts of the service that I usually covered so that I would have as much voice left for the sermon as possible.

Eventually things got so bad that I had to resign for the sake of the church. I didn't want to be the reason that the church went under.

Which brings me around to the purpose for this book. For seventeen or eighteen years, I would spend a good part of my week preparing a message to deliver to the church. It was easily my favorite part of what I did as a pastor. I would study a passage from the Bible, God would deal with me through His Word, I would prepare a sermon, and on Sunday morning I would deliver it. It's a simple and profoundly mysterious process that repeats itself in thousands of churches around the world.

And then all of a sudden, that process was taken away from me.

So this book is an expedition in search of my voice. Not my actual voice, although there is always the possibility that it may return, but a search for a new voice.

God is still dealing with me, and I still have things I am learning and stories to tell and I am afraid that if I don't find an outlet, my head will explode!

The transition out of ministry was a wild ride. I began looking for a job for the first time since college. I became an Uber driver, we went in search of a new church to attend, and we did some serious faith walking.

I would like to thank Barb for keeping up the gentle pressure on me to put these experiences on paper. By her estimation, she made around four hundred gentle suggestions, prods, and encouragements. She convinced me that my stories were interesting and that I had the skill to tell them in a way that would be fun and encouraging for you. I hope she is right.

As an Uber driver, I gave rides to people from all different walks of life, including prostitutes, exotic dancers, men dressed as women, drug addicts, gangbangers and drunks. It's quite possible that you may find some of these stories offensive, and for that I apologize. However, I contend that a few Friday nights driving for Uber would be good for most of us. We would have a clearer understanding of this world's broken condition.

God's Classroom

FROM 1980 UNTIL I STEPPED down from ministry because of the problems with my voice, I had six jobs. Technically, two of the positions were with the same church, so I worked in five places, all churches, all ministries, in thirty-five years. But then my health issues suddenly sent me searching for a job outside the walls of the church, and in the words of the artist formerly known as Cat Stevens—"Ooh, baby, baby, it's a wild world."

I stopped counting after submitting my application and resume twenty times in just two weeks.

Everything is done online now, and I had so many sign-in accounts and passwords that I needed a computer program just to keep track of everything. Some of the submitted applications generated a response—typically a robotic email that indicated that I had successfully completed the application process, but I shouldn't get my hopes up because there was no one at the other end of the internet to call or ask questions. In other words, "Don't call us—we'll call you." And some, if not most, of my electronic forms were routed to a virtual shredder at some server farm and were being used as bedding for virtual server farm animals.

I am a firm believer in the concept that God uses every situation and circumstance to teach us something. I am convinced that He has each of us on a specific curriculum that is tailored to shape us and mold us into who He wants us to become, and until we learn the lessons at the level we are on, we stay there. I had preached that concept more times than I could count. I had used it in counseling situations and with people who were dealing with trouble. And now I was about to see if I believed what I had been espousing. I had to ask myself the glaring question, "What am I supposed to be learning?"

"Is the lesson about humility, Lord?" One day I got a rejection email from a major supermarket chain in response to my application for the deli clerk position. The application questions had been typical—"Are you over eighteen? Do you possess a high school diploma/GED? Are you a US citizen?" The only other question was what I thought to be a strange inquiry—"Are you able to wear a hairnet?" Maybe some people can't, but I remember answering yes, I could, albeit reluctantly, wear a hairnet. Was the hairnet question my downfall? It was a humbling experience.

Was the lesson on patience? According to the schedule in my head, I should have been gainfully employed in just a few weeks. I should have been scooped up by the first company or organization that heard I was available. The reality was that the process was painfully slow and frustrating. I had applied for several positions with a federal entity that offers express delivery, but that guarantee of speedy service did not apply to their ability to make timely hiring decisions. Did I need a refresher course in patience?

Was the lesson on contentment? I had a lot of experience in leadership and team building. I could work with people from all kinds of backgrounds and mediate a crisis. But all of those things depended almost entirely on being able to speak clearly and consistently. I could see pretty quickly that I was going to take a major hit in the income department. Had I become too dependent on money? Did I need to be dropped down a few notches and relearn how to be content with less?

That season was God's classroom for me. He was preparing me, not for graduation, but for the next lesson in His curriculum plan. I clearly had more to learn.

Looking back on those first few months when everything was turning upside down, I realize now that I had a critical decision to make. I could resist the process that God was asking me to enter, or I could take my own advice and accept what I was going through as God at work in my life.

God does not stir up chaos in our lives for fun. He uses the pain and the struggle and the victory and the triumph to move us closer to what we are supposed to be.

There seems to be no way around it. We learn most effectively in the trenches as we live our struggles.

I can't say I like very much what James says in chapter 1, verses 2–4, but I can't fault the spiritual logic:

Consider it pure joy my brothers and sisters, whenever you face trials of many kinds, because you know that the testing of your faith produces perseverance. Let perseverance finish its work so that you may be mature, not lacking anything. (James 1:2-4)

***

After my thirty-five years of church ministry came to a close, my full-time job became driving for the ride-sharing services Uber and Lyft. Using Uber or Lyft is a lot like taking a taxi—except it usually smells better.

Here's how it would work if you got a ride from me: You download the Uber or Lyft app to your smartphone and go online to order a ride. Somehow the app knows where you are, and if I am working and happen to be the closest driver to your location, my phone chimes. Then I have fifteen seconds to decide if I want to accept the ride request. I can't begin to tell you how pressure packed those fifteen seconds are. If I accept the request, my driver app navigates me to where you are, and most of the time we find each other without much trouble. You get in the front seat or the back seat, and then I start the trip and find out where we are going. If you have entered a destination, my phone navigates me there, or you could give me progressive directions, or you could just say something like "Amtrak Station please," assuming I know how to get there.

I drive you to your destination, your credit card on file with the company automatically pays the fare, you give me a tip (hopefully), and we both continue the journey we call life. It's a pretty slick system.

There are slight variations between ride-sharing apps, but they work very similarly. For the sake of simplicity, I will refer to all my ride-sharing activities as "Ubering." I suppose Uber is to ride sharing what Kleenex is to facial tissue. You don't ask someone to hand you a Kirkland facial tissue. You say, "Could you hand me a Kleenex please?" But when you blow your nose, you don't refer to that as "Kleenexing," so the comparison only goes so far.

One of the decisions I made when I started Ubering was to be honest with people if it came up in conversation what I did before Uber. It came up often, so I simply said, "For the past thirty-five years, I have been a pastor." At that point one of three things would normally happen.

First, the ride might continue in awkward silence. Even if I tried to jumpstart the conversation, my declaration that I was "a man of the cloth" was a buzzkill. I'm not sure why this happened. Maybe because of the way pastors are portrayed on television or in the movies. They might have had negative experiences with the church at some point. I don't know, but it was a pretty typical response.

Or when I identified myself as a pastor, the person(s) became apologetic because I had just picked them up at a nightclub, or they had been using profanity, or from her phone conversation it was obvious that she was a prostitute. There was no small amount of stammering and backpedaling. One guy called me "Father" for the rest of the trip.

The third response—and it didn't happen every day, or even every week—was the feeling that I was entering into a divine appointment with a complete stranger.

They had a tough question to ask that they thought I might be qualified to answer, or an important relationship was strained and they hoped I could offer a word of advice. Or they had some need that was weighing them down, and they were looking for a little bit of encouragement, even from a former pastor who was currently exiled to driving for Uber. One night, I picked up a couple from a local hospital who had just watched as his mother was removed from life support after a severe stroke had left her mind and body ravaged. When we arrived at their destination, I asked if I could pray for them. Moments like this were rare, but no one ever said no.

As strange as it may sound, and as odd as it might have looked to a person walking by, praying with a total stranger about their deepest needs and fears and hopes seemed to be the most natural thing in the world.

Most of the time, Ubering was just driving people where they needed to be. But sometimes—once in a while—it was something more.

CHAPTER 1

You're Not the Driver

"Worry implies that we don't quite trust that God is big enough, powerful enough, or loving enough to take care of what's happening in our lives." —Francis Chan

MOST PEOPLE WHO HAVE BEEN drinking think that they are funny and charming, but in reality, they are usually just louder and more obnoxious. The couple I picked up from a wine-tasting event at the Del Rio Country Club was a rare exception.

They had me laughing out loud in the front seat. They were like George Burns and Gracie Allen. Their timing was impeccable. She would feed him a line, and he would deliver the punch. He would do an impression of Sean Penn, and she would become Madonna, singing the chorus of "Girls Just Want to Have Fun." It was like they had rehearsed their act.

We came around a corner and drove right into a sobriety checkpoint.

I find DUI checkpoints fascinating and exciting. They are always set up on a major street leading out of an area where there is a high concentration of drinking establishments. They are strategically placed where you won't see them as you approach, like around a corner, or just over a hill. There are patrol cars everywhere with all their lights flashing. Orange cones funnel the traffic into a single-file line. All the possible routes of avoidance are guarded by motorcycle officers who will chase down anyone who decides to take another way home. They stop about ten cars at a time under these incredibly intense lights, and people are running around everywhere, and the police officers are in full uniform with reflective vests and their service weapons. It's like a circus.

But my guy in the back seat, who just a minute ago was doing a spot-on Bill Clinton impression, was in trouble. I glanced in the mirror and noticed that he had slid down in his seat, and all I could see was the top of his head. I adjusted the mirror and saw that he had a look of abject terror on his face. His eyes were twitching from left to right as he realized that we were trapped.

The orange cones were forcing us into a line, and the motorcycle officers had the exits covered. The bright lights were like all-seeing eyes that would expose his condition. His instincts were screaming for him to run—to abandon his wife and to flee into the darkness of the almond orchards.

So I turned around and looked into my passenger's panic-stricken eyes and said, "Hey, buddy. Relax. It's okay. You're not driving. I am."

You could see the alcohol-impaired wheels slowly spinning in his brain. There was a glimmer of comprehension on his face.

"I'm not driving . . . you are," He echoed back.

"You have nothing to worry about because you are not behind the wheel," I said in the most reassuring voice I had.

"I'm not going to get a DUI because I'm not driving." He sat back up, almost straight. His breathing slowed, and a smile formed on his face. It was the smile of someone who had just placed a bet and won.

When it was my turn to pull into one of the ten or so positions, the officer took my ID, but she didn't even look at it. She had spotted the sticker in the front window that identified my vehicle as an Uber car.

She addressed me as Mr. Uber and said, "How are you doing this evening?" I kept both hands on the steering wheel and said, "It's a Friday night, so business is good."

She directed her flashlight into the back seat, where my passengers were sitting with goofy grins on their faces. The officer returned my license, thanked me for getting these folks home safely, and waved us through.

The remainder of the trip included no comedy routine or singing or impressions. A few miles later, I dropped my riders at their home. They said "Thank you," and I commended them on choosing an Uber over driving. I could not resist making the point that the eight or ten dollar fare was considerably cheaper than a DUI.

As I drove away in search of my next passengers, I supposed we had all learned something. My lesson was a reminder that as tempting as it is to sit in life's driver's seat, it's much wiser and safer to let someone more qualified take that role.

While I can be trusted to drive a drunk couple home, when it comes to life, I'm definitely the guy with the impaired thought process who is on the verge of total panic when the stuff hits the fan. I'm the guy who freaks out when life turns a corner and the unexpected is right there: a crisis or a change or a disappointment. My instincts tell me to run screaming into the almond orchards.

But then my admittedly slow wheels begin to turn, and God reminds me to relax. "You're not driving . . . I AM"

Off Course with a Child of the '60s . . . Sort Of

The first time my route veered far from my expectations, I had only been Ubering for a few weeks. I was in Turlock, and I got a ride request from someone in Oakdale, about thirty miles away.

The problem was I didn't know where the rider wanted to go. You see, the way the Uber driver app works, you don't know the rider's destination until they get into your car. You flick a button on your smartphone that says Start Trip, which causes a map to appear with your current location and the destination the rider has entered, connected by a red line.

I get why the people at Uber designed the program that way—so drivers wouldn't "shop" for their favorite kind of trips, leaving everyone else standing along the road waiting for a ride.

I took a chance on my Oakdale guy and drove the thirty miles, hoping he would want more than a ride across town (Oakdale is not all that big). We met up in a grocery store parking lot, and my first impression was that he looked as if he had stepped directly out of 1967, even though he could not have been more than thirty or thirty-five years old. He was wearing a macramé hat, round wire-rimmed glasses, a tie-dyed shirt, and Birkenstock sandals. Next to him on the ground was a bedroll attached to an old-fashioned, external-frame backpack.

As I helped him load his stuff into my car, he informed me that he had been at a five-day festival called Symbiosis Gathering at the Woodward Reservoir Regional Park.

"I've never heard of that," I replied. "What was it about?"

He said, "It's kind of like Burning Man, but with a little less nudity and drugs."

This was going to be an interesting trip.

He piled into the back seat along with a couple of his personal items. I readied my finger on the Start Trip slider, hoping that I would be making enough money to cover at least the cost of gas getting to Oakdale. I flicked my finger and the map appeared. It was a map of the entire North-Central San Joaquin Valley and San Francisco Bay Area with a red line from Oakdale to the Haight-Ashbury District in San Francisco. It was at least a hundred-mile trip one way.

"Holy crap! You want to go to San Francisco?" That may not be exactly what I said, but whatever I said, I said out loud.

"Is that going to be a problem?"

I said "No," but the truth was, I didn't have cash for the bridge toll, or enough gas in the tank to get home from San Francisco.

We stopped at a cash machine on our way out of Oakdale, and as we settled in for the drive west, I asked him more about the Symbiosis Gathering. "So what was the festival all about that you went to?"

"It's kind of hard to explain," he told me. "It's a community of artists and musicians who are into self-expression and sustainability."

I responded with a thoughtful "hmmm," but I really didn't have any idea what he was talking about.

"They have seminars and workshops during the days," he continued. "I went to a class on organic farming and one about civil disobedience. My favorite workshop was on how to make your own clothes."

That explained his hat.

"It sounds like an interesting, um, event," I said, smiling into the rearview mirror.

"Oh, it was so great. Last night was the closing party, and we danced around the fire until this morning."

That earned an admiring "wow" from me.

As conversation continued, I found out that he was from Portland, Oregon, and that he had a flight out of the San Francisco Airport that left at 11:00 p.m.

"My app says that you are going downtown. The airport is quite a ways from where I am dropping you off," I warned.

"I'll just get another Uber to the airport later," he explained. "Visiting the Haight-Ashbury is kind of a pilgrimage for me. I wish that I had been born in the '60s."

I thought I was really connecting with this guy. "I am from the Portland area, too. Not downtown or anything. I grew up out in the country outside of Portland, and I was born in 1960."

After a long pause, I looked in the back seat. He had tipped over onto his hemp tote bag and was sound asleep. The remainder of the trip was spent in contemplative silence.

On every trip, when I flipped that button in the Uber app, I felt a twinge of terror—and excitement. I could be going across town—or across the state.

I had a passenger tell me once that the day before, her driver claimed to have just returned from delivering a pair of college guys to Las Vegas, Nevada! I don't know if that is a true story or an Uber urban legend, but following my experience with my wannabe child of the '60s, I would keep my gas tank at least half full and carry money for emergencies.

As we crossed the Oakland Bay Bridge and neared the destination, the sun was setting over San Francisco and my passenger remained comfortably asleep in the back seat. It was a beautiful scene, one that naturally invited deep thought.

I had made my plans for the future based on reasonable assumptions. I thought I would continue in church work well into my "golden years," maybe completing the circle of ministry that began with working with students by finding a church that needed a seniors pastor. Or maybe I would preach a powerful message and then drop dead behind the pulpit to emphasize my final point.

But I had recently been reminded that life can turn on a dime—and it often does. Nobody expects a simple doctor's appointment for a twitching pinky finger to reveal a disease that will change everything.

As we took our exit from the bridge, I surveyed the situation. Oakdale to San Francisco, a sleeping millennial who wished he was a hippie in my back seat, and the prospect of a long, lonely drive back home. I had flipped the Start Trip switch on a new phase of the journey.

Driving in Circles

Motivational speaker and author Zig Ziglar famously said, "If you aim at nothing, you will hit it every time." If I understand him correctly, he is saying that if you don't have a goal or a priority or a destination in mind, you will wander around aimlessly, which is the basic job description of an Uber driver.

On a handful of occasions, I decided to leave my local territory around Modesto and head for the mythical land of nonstop riders and higher fares and big money. I had met several other drivers who told me tales of driving in San Francisco and being so busy making money that they didn't have time to stop for lunch! I tried the big city two or three times, but as it turns out, I like to have time to stop for lunch.

I did make more money driving in San Francisco, but the volume of traffic was absolutely insane. People drive like they are demon possessed, and if you need to use the restroom, forget about finding a place to park near a public one. I once paid $14.00 for an order of nachos so that I was a customer and eligible to get the code to use the bathroom.

One day, I decided to try a compromise between the comfort and familiarity of the Modesto area and the chaos of the big city. I got up early and drove to San Leandro, a city on the east side of the San Francisco Bay. I left my Uber app turned off because I wanted to get to my planned starting point without being pulled off course. I waited until exactly 7:00 a.m. and started Ubering.

To my delight, I was pinged for a ride within just a minute or two. I drove a couple of miles and picked up a young man who was headed for work. When I accepted the ride and pushed the Start Trip button, his destination was a PetSmart in Pleasanton, which was about twenty miles back in the direction I had just come from. It was not what I had planned, but he was a paying customer.

My next rider was close by, at a Hilton Garden Hotel. He worked for a major auto parts store and was in town visiting the company franchises, starting that day in Santa Clara, down at the south end of the bay, near San Jose. So far I was batting zero in my plan to work in San Leandro.

We got on the freeway heading toward the south bay and traffic was a nightmare. I could feel his frustration building with every mile as we started and stopped our way toward his destination. "Get out in the express lanes," he urged. "The traffic is moving a lot faster over there."

"I don't have a FasTrak transponder for use in the express lanes, and all I would accomplish in those lanes would be to get a fistful of lane violation tickets."

By the time we reached his meeting, I could see the veins in his forehead. He got out and emphatically slammed my car door. I assumed that I would not be getting a tip.

I got a request in San Jose that took me to a house in a nice neighborhood. To my surprise, the passengers were a couple of kids. A girl, maybe nine or ten, and a boy, who looked to be in the first or second grade. They were dressed in school uniforms and waiting in the driveway like I was the school bus or something. "Are you waiting for an Uber?" I asked as I pulled up to them.

The girl said, "Yes," so I reached back and opened the door for them.

They were dressed for school, but I asked the obvious question anyway. "Am I driving you to school?"

The girl, who seemed to be speaking for both of them, said, "Yes."

This was such a unique situation that I was determined to find out what was going on. I asked the spokesperson, "Do you take an Uber to school every day, or is this a special occasion?"

She must have been under orders to talk as little as possible to the Uber driver, because all she said was, "Every day."

Their private school was only about ten minutes from their house. The girl directed me to a line of cars that I would need to get into in order to drop them off. I looked around, and my car was easily the oldest and ugliest in the line.

I felt like I should say something as they got out of the car, but all I could think of was, "Have a nice day at school." They didn't look back or say anything. I just had time to think, *What is this world coming to when a parent would send their children alone in a car with a complete stranger?* Before I could give it any more thought, my phone told me I had another rider.

My destination was the Tesla assembly plant in Fremont. I had a bit of trouble finding my rider because it was a shift change and the parking lot was crowded with cars and people, but we connected and headed for his house.

To my surprise, the Uber app started indicating that I had another ride request while I was in the middle of delivering my Tesla guy home. He noticed my confusion and said, "Go ahead and accept the ride."

It turns out that in big markets, like the Bay Area, a rider can choose to share his or her ride with another person who is going in the same general direction, and the riders get to split the cost of the trip. It was interesting and fairly embarrassing to have my passenger explain how to do my job.

A few rides later, I picked up a man who was on his way to the San Francisco Airport to catch a flight to Paris. He had been visiting the main campus of his employer, GoPro action cameras. I had owned several GoPros, and he was very interested in how I used his company's products and what I thought of them. He had a large carry-on bag, and I inquired, "Are you giving away any product samples today?"

He had a good laugh, but I said, "I'm serious. You must keep a few cameras handy to give out to Uber drivers, right?"

He unzipped a side pocket on his bag and my heart started beating faster, but he handed me a sticker of the GoPro company logo. It was worth a shot.

I realized that I had not thought about my failed plan to work in San Leandro for a couple of hours. I was just letting the ride requests chart my course, and it was fun. Each segment of the trip was a new adventure.

I kept being pulled north by my ride requests until I was, once again, in the land of fourteen-dollar nachos. I picked up a guy wearing a baby blue tuxedo from a restaurant, accompanied by his adorable five-year-old twin sons in identical tuxes. They were going to the courthouse, where the dad was going to be married with his boys sharing the role of best man.

After I delivered the groom and his best men to the courthouse, I turned the wrong way down a one-way street and marveled at the friendly drivers who honked and waved.

I got creative and used the bathroom at a high school basketball game by just walking in and pretending like I belonged there. I bought a bag of peanut M&M's for a dollar at the concession table on my way out because I felt guilty, but I still saved thirteen dollars.

My last ride of the day was two couples who crammed into my car headed for dinner at a Beacon Hill eatery. We became mired in near-gridlocked traffic because, according to one of my passengers, I made the mistake of following the route provided by the Uber app. One of the women suggested that they might make better time walking. I chuckled, but they were serious. They opened their doors and piled out of the car right in the middle of the street. The last guy out handed me a couple of dollars, and I watched as the group of four pulled away from me on the sidewalk.

It was getting dark, and I had been up since around 4:30 a.m., so I decided to call it a day. Traffic was horrendous most of the way home, which provided ample time to think.

I had started with a plan in mind, which had immediately gone down the toilet with my first rider. For the first couple hours, I felt the need to get back to San Leandro, but when it became clear that I was not in control of the situation, I resolved to simply enjoy the ride.

I had taken aim at my target and missed completely, but instead of hitting nothing, I met some interesting people, had some mild adventures and a few close calls, and made more money in one day driving in circles around the San Francisco Bay than I usually made in two good days back around home.

There is a time and place for buckling down and hitting targets, and there is also a certain amount of joy in relaxing and enjoying the ride. This lesson applies to life in general as well as to Ubering. Even when things are not going as planned and I am being pulled off course by setbacks and unexpected changes, I can sense God working in the background, orchestrating His plan while mine falls apart.

Looking back, I had the opportunity to share my story with people I never would have known otherwise. I met people and ministered to people that I would have never crossed paths with if my plans had worked out. And I had some adventures that certainly would have never happened if I had not surrendered and hung on for the ride.

He's Got Your Back

Sometimes I wonder if God is big enough to handle all the prayers and problems of the whole world, all at once. My theology says "yes," but my limited mind has a hard time believing it. I think we just need God to remind us that He is still in charge—that He is big enough to pay attention to our circumstances and everyone else's, all at once.

I picked up two young men and their giant laundry bag full of clothes in Modesto. My guess was that they were going back to their dorm or apartment after doing laundry at mom and dad's place. But when I started their trip, to my surprise, we were headed for San Bruno, a city just down the peninsula from San Francisco.

The trip west was uneventful and the traffic was light, but I could see that the traffic headed back toward Modesto was pure chaos, so I decided to work in the area for a few hours while the traffic died down a little. I would quit around dark and head for home with an empty car, because the odds of stumbling upon someone in San Bruno who wanted to go to Modesto were astronomically small.

Once I had dropped the two passengers off at their destination, I started pinging for a ride. I got one almost immediately. She called me as soon as I accepted the ride. She had just gotten off the CalTrain at the San Bruno station, she explained, and was in the parking lot.

"Pull into the station," she suggested in a strong Indian accent, "and we can figure out how to find each other."

As I pulled into the crowded parking area, I saw a woman talking on her phone. I said, "Are you wearing a blue blouse?"

She confirmed that she was and said, "Flash your headlights so I know which car is you."

I flashed my headlights, and she flashed back a pretty smile and waved. She got in the back seat, and I did what I always do when driving outside my home area: I confessed that I was from out of town and would appreciate any help with navigation. She expertly guided me out of the station, into a U-turn lane, and onto the main street toward her home.

She seemed very interested in my situation. "If you are not from this area, where are you from?" she asked.

"I'm from Modesto," I told her, "over in the valley." But she had never heard of Modesto. I told her about the laundry-toting boys that I had dropped off in San Bruno and that I was planning to drive locally for a while.

"How long are you planning to work in the San Francisco area?" she asked.

All the questions were starting to make me a little nervous. "I'm not really sure. A couple of hours maybe. I want to let the traffic die down a little on the freeways."

I heard the click of a seat belt being unbuckled. I turned my head and tried to see what she was doing. "Um, Miss. You need to stay buckled in."

She moved to the center in the back and stuck her head between the bucket seats. "Did you know that there is a way, when out of your home area, to get help from the app with finding riders that are headed in the direction you want to go?"

"I didn't know that," I confessed.

She said, "Hand me your phone. I will show you."

The phone was clipped into the center air vent on my dashboard and easy to remove. I handed it to her over my shoulder. She expertly navigated through several screens while giving me instructions.

"So here is where you live, correct?" She pointed to Modesto on the map. "And here we are in San Bruno. When you get ready to go back to Modesto, just choose a city that is on your way home and the app will search for riders headed in the same direction."

I finally asked her if she drove for Uber and she said, "No." She was actually a senior software engineer for Uber and she and her team designed the app I was using!

I said, "*Shut up!*"

Of course I didn't say that; she worked for the company that paid my wages. I did thank her for her help, and she thanked me for all my hard work out there driving for Uber.

My very next rider was an elderly woman, waiting for me on the corner in front of another townhouse complex. After she got into the car, I gave my "not from this area" speech, and she looked panicked.

She was visiting her son from out of town. She didn't know the area and could provide no help at all. Fortunately, her son had requested the trip and provided their dinner destination and a corresponding route.

As we headed for the freeway, I made some small talk. "Where are you from?" I had noticed that her English was excellent, but she had a strong accent.

"I am from Turkey," she replied. I whipped my head toward the rearview mirror and told her that my wife and I had been in Turkey just a few weeks ago visiting our son and daughter-in-law who are missionaries.

She said, "*Shut up!*"

I'm kidding of course, but she was thrilled and very curious about our impressions of her country. It turned out that she was from Izmir, a city we had visited. She asked if we had taken in the ancient city of Ephesus, which we had, and she explained that she and her husband had a summer home in Selcuk.

I said, "*Shut up!*" (Kidding.) "We spent the night in Selcuk!"

We spent the rest of the ride laughing and in wonder that the world was so small.

I turned my new friend over to her son at a restaurant in Burlingame and she spoke to him in Turkish, explaining, I presume our love for their homeland, which generated smiles, handshakes, "thank yous," and a nice tip.

It was starting to get dark, so I set up my app to find people headed east, just like my software engineer friend had taught me. I was somewhat successful and had paying customers for at least part of the drive.

As I traveled home, I thought about how easy it is sometimes to assume that with all God has to think about and take care of He couldn't possibly have the time to deal with my situation, too. But of all the people he could have put in my car, he chose a software engineer who was eager to help me do my job more successfully, followed by a Turkish woman who lived in the very place where Barb and I had been just a few weeks prior.

It was as if He was smiling and saying, "Don't worry Steve. I've got your back."

CHAPTER 2

Steering through Crises

Anti-Lock Brakes

I CONCLUDED VERY EARLY IN MY career as an Uber driver that there were quite a few people who should never have been issued a motor vehicle license. I'm not saying that I am an exceptional driver, or even an above-average one. It's just that when your job is driving, you see things that make you wish it were much harder to get a driver's license. But I don't want this chapter to become a rant against people who should only be allowed to use public transportation. I have a much more redemptive story to tell.

I was flipping through TV channels one day at home and came across one of those "How Things Work" kind of shows. The subject was automotive anti-lock braking systems, or ABS. The show had already started, but what was happening on the screen was fascinating.

There were two cars of similar size and weight roaring down a test track at about sixty miles per hour. They both crossed a yellow line on the pavement and slammed on their brakes. The car without anti-lock brakes was decidedly more fun to watch as smoke poured off of the tires and the professional driver behind the wheel, who almost certainly did not ride the bus to work, struggled to keep the car under control. But you had to appreciate the difference as the car equipped with ABS came to a smooth stop in about two-thirds the distance the other car took.

The narrator went on to explain how the anti-lock braking system works. Modern cars are equipped with sensors and decelerometers that can tell the difference between normal, or even hard-braking, situations and all-out, both-feet-on-the-brake-pedal, panic stops.

When the brake is depressed hard enough, valves open and close and mechanically "tap" the brakes up to fifteen times per second. The system monitors the progress of the stop and makes constant adjustments that ensure maximum braking efficiency, while not allowing the wheels to lock up. Thus the clever name—anti-lock brakes.

The most amazing part about this technology is that while the ABS is trying like crazy to get the vehicle stopped, the driver can still effectively steer the car!

They demonstrated this on the television program by sending another car driven by someone who had not ridden the bus to work speeding down the track toward a line of orange safety cones. Just before plowing into the first cone, the driver slammed on the brakes, and like an Olympic downhill slalom skier, maneuvered the car between the cones, missing each one by mere inches, until the car came to an abrupt stop on the other side of the line of cones.

I completed driver's education in high school and got my driver's license in the mid-seventies. This was the pre-ABS era, and the conventional wisdom at the time involved learning how to "control a skid." A skid was the result of hitting a patch of ice or going too fast around a corner or slamming on the brakes in a vain attempt to avoid a collision.

The rule was to "turn in the direction of the skid," which, as it turns out, was a lie from the pit of hell and served only as something to keep drivers occupied while they waited for impact with whatever it was they were trying to avoid. But now, over forty years later, I was finally armed with detailed knowledge about anti-lock brakes, and it was only a couple of weeks later that I had the opportunity to use this newfound information.

I picked up a couple who was headed for a restaurant in the downtown area from their home in Modesto. They were chatting in the back seat as we entered a left turn lane with a green arrow indicating that we were clear to enter an intersection known as "Five Corners." (I know, it doesn't make sense to me either.) But as we began our turn, I noticed movement to my right. A midsized sedan of some kind was blowing through a red light into an intersection already busy with two lanes of traffic turning left from opposite directions, and he appeared to not have a care in the world.

I remember having two distinct thoughts at that moment. First, I wished that this guy had taken public transportation to wherever he was going, and second, we were either going to hit another car or be hit by one.

I slammed on the brakes and immediately felt the pedal vibrating rapidly, an indication that the anti-lock brakes were doing what they do, but we were on a collision course with the car that was running the light.

Then, in a moment of clarity, I remembered the television program and the guy driving slalom style while making a panic stop. I turned hard right, slipped behind the car we were headed for, and came to a stop just past the middle of the intersection. We just sat there for a few seconds until I remembered I had passengers in the car. All I could think to say was "Sorry about that."

The guy in back said, "It wasn't your fault. That guy was an idiot."

I was tempted to give them a detailed explanation of how anti-lock brakes work, but I opted to go around the block and get them to their restaurant in silence.

Something to note is that since the introduction of anti-lock brakes, there are still car accidents. Even with constantly improving safety features, people figure out ways to crash their cars. Anti-lock brakes simply give drivers another tool to hopefully prevent an accident.

When things started going badly with my health, I realized pretty quickly that the situation was out of my control. There is no cure for Parkinson's Disease, only treatments that become more viable as things get more serious.

One of the few options I had, and continue to have, is to choose my response to my circumstances. I could turn in the direction of the skid and hope for the best, letting the situation control my attitudes and actions. Or I could put the situation in God's hands and trust Him for the outcome—much like I trusted my ABS in that intersection.

Uber Improv

When I was growing up, our family would go tent camping, usually in Eastern Oregon. I think my parents' strategy was to get on the east side of the Cascade Mountains, where it was warmer and rained less.

One of the places we went several times was Lake Simtustus, the reservoir created by Pelton Dam, near Madras, Oregon. I have good memories of that place: swimming in the lake, sliding down a grassy slope on pieces of cardboard, and roasting marshmallows over the fire late into the evening.

Another vivid memory I have of Pelton Park involves a group of young women who were camping in the space next to our family. The girls were minding their own business when a carload of boys, probably from a neighboring town, pulled up to their campsite and started giving them trouble. They wanted the girls to go with them, probably to a party or into town.

The details are kind of sketchy in my mind. However, I vividly remember what my dad did. He picked up the axe we had brought along for chopping firewood and walked over to the carload of boys and encouraged them to move along.

They wondered noisily about what jurisdiction he had over the girls. My dad just said that one of the girls was his daughter and the rest were her friends and that they should leave. He stared them down, axe in hand, for a few seconds, and then they spun their tires in protest and left in a cloud of dust and loose gravel.

I looked at my dad differently from that day forward. My dad could be menacing. An axe-wielding, potentially crazy guy who just might go all "lumberjack" on a carload of local boys cruising for chicks. And under certain circumstances, he could improvise. Not one of those girls was my sister.

One night I was Ubering the swing shift when a ride request came just before midnight. Three early-high-school-age girls were on a midnight Slurpee and chocolate run to the local 7-Eleven, which in my opinion was in a very bad neighborhood. The first question that came to mind: Do any of these girls' parents know what they are up to? A call from one of their mothers putting in an order for something chocolate with almonds answered that concern. The other question: If something should go sideways at the 7-Eleven, what is my duty as the only adult present?

The girls were loud and goofy. They included me in their conversation, which is fairly rare, but they were polite and I didn't sense any disrespect from them at all.

We pulled into the 7-Eleven lot, which was completely empty, and I parked directly in front of the door so I had a clear view of the cash register. The girls got out and headed for the Slurpee machine while I tapped my foot and willed them to hurry up so I could deliver them home and off my hands.

Then it happened. A "tweaker" on a BMX-style bike designed for a twelve-year-old zipped up, dumped the bike, and went inside. I'm no expert on drug abuse, but I had been working late at night in downtown Modesto long enough to know a tweaker when I saw one.

Tweakers are heavy methamphetamine users. Generally speaking, they tend to be compulsive, unpredictable, prone to violence, and very twitchy. The Urban Dictionary has this comparison as part of the definition for "tweaker": "What's the difference between a crackhead and a tweaker? The crackhead will steal your [stuff] and bounce—the tweaker will steal your [stuff] and then help you look for it."

I watched from the car as the situation unfolded and observed in horror as my worst fear materialized. Everyone brought their selections to the cashier at the same time. There were words being exchanged, and then the tweaker put his arm around one of the girls. Not in a chokehold kind of way, but more of a "How you doin'?" kind of way.

I had no axe, but something had to be done. There was no Uber Code of Conduct manual that covered a situation like this, so I improvised. I got out of the car, put on my most menacing expression, flung open the door, and said, "Get your hands off my daughter!"

They all just stared in disbelief. The cashier, the girls . . . and the tweaker. And to my great surprise and relief, he did remove his arm. I said, "Pay for your [stuff] and let's go." They did, and we left.

There were lots of good-natured laughs at my expense in the car. One of the girls suggested that "Get your hands off my granddaughter" might have been more believable. Ha ha. I was still shaking like a tweaker.

When we got back to where I had picked them up, I encouraged the girls to be careful because it's a crazy world out there. The last one out turned and said, "Thanks, *Dad*."

I grew up in a culture where people looked out for each other, where neighbors kept an eye on who was snooping around. There was an unwritten rule that said you had an obligation to step in and get involved, especially if there were women and children at risk.

Sure, I made a fool of myself when I burst into the 7-Eleven, but I took it right out of my dad's playbook—and I think he might have been proud.

Scared Straight

I once picked up a pair of passengers who used a term that I was unfamiliar with: "predrinking." I didn't ask for an explanation, but as they continued to talk, the definition became apparent. Predrinking is basically getting a head start on becoming drunk before heading out to a bar or restaurant to finish the job.

The decision to predrink is primarily a matter of finances. I learned that in some bars and clubs, a single high-end cocktail can cost as much as fourteen dollars! When I heard that fact, I instantly did the math in my head and calculated that Barb and I could eat dinner at Taco Bell one and a half times for the price of one mixed drink, which is a commentary on the outrageous markup on cocktails and the quality of the food at Taco Bell.

So to save money, people buy inexpensive liquor or everyday beer, drink it at home, and then call an Uber to take them someplace where they can complete the task.

I picked up a group of four young people, two guys and two girls, who were probably in their very early twenties. They had been "predrinking." I could smell it on their breath and detect it in their behavior. They were a bit loud and jocular. They were all trying to talk at the same time. They were excited to be heading into town for some celebration of a new weekend.

I was busy confirming their destination and was not paying attention to their conversation, but when I did tune in to them, I was shocked. The subject they were discussing was unbelievably vulgar and graphic and should not have been talked about in mixed company, let alone in the presence of a stranger.

It was impossible to not hear what they were saying, but I was determined to just be the driver, get them to their destination, and move on. But then something completely unexpected and horrifying happened. The rider up front, a young woman, attempted to drag me into the discussion. She asked me an entirely inappropriate question that was so vulgar and disturbing that I was completely at a loss to respond.

In the late seventies, I watched a documentary called *Scared Straight*. It was directed by Arnold Shapiro and narrated by actor Peter Falk (Columbo). It centers on a group of juvenile delinquents who spend a three-hour session with actual convicts who are housed at the Rathway State Prison in New Jersey. In the film, a group of inmates known as the "Lifers" berate, scream at, and terrify the young offenders in an attempt to "scare them straight" (hence the film's title), so that the teenagers will avoid prison life.

I had picked up my passengers out in the country northwest of Modesto around 9:00 p.m., and we were traveling through almond orchards and farmhouses, so it was a pretty good place to do what I did. I will admit that I didn't think my plan through completely, or at all. I just did it.

I stepped on the brakes—too hard—and swung the car off of the pavement and onto the gravel shoulder. We jerked to a stop, and a cloud of dust enveloped the car and swirled in the headlights. It was quiet now, except for the radio. I said, "Get out of my car."

Now you should know: I may not have thought things through, but I did not intend to abandon my passengers on a dark stretch of country road lined with orchards. I was hoping, however, to make a point.

After a few seconds of silence and an awkward chuckle or two, one of the guys in the back seat spoke up: "What do you mean get out? Here?"

I told them again, "I want you all out of my car . . . right now. This is my personal car. I am not an employee of Uber. I am a contract worker for Uber, but I am not under any obligation to be harassed or degraded by any passenger who treats me the way I have been handled by you four. According to my contract with Uber, if I feel unsafe at any time, I have the right to eject a rider from my car, ending the ride. The only stipulation is that I let you out in a safe place. This looks like a safe place. Now get out!"

I wish you could have been there. It was like the final scene of *Scared Straight*. There were multiple apologies and some tearful pleading. They blamed their behavior on predrinking and youthful carelessness. They backpedaled and made solemn promises and vows of purity. The young woman who asked me the very vulgar question was particularly upset and begged me to forgive her. She seemed genuinely upset for "breaking the camel's back," so to speak. She called me "sir," and through her tears she told me how sorry she was for offending me. It was really fun.

By this time, I was having trouble keeping a straight face, but I managed to stay in character. I had begun to consider the consequences of my actions if my riders chose to report the incident to Uber. I made up most of the stuff about my rights as a driver and my option to leave them on the roadside in the dark.

I preemptively threatened to file a report with Uber detailing their behavior and explained that their verbal abuse of a driver might lead to the deactivation of their account. As far as I know, it was all empty threats, but they seemed convinced.

We got back on our way, and except for the radio, the rest of the ride was silent. When we got to their destination, a bar in downtown Modesto, they each added a few more words of apology and thanked me for not leaving them stranded.

I realize that some would disagree with my decision to threaten the "nuclear option" right from the start. I could have tried a stern talking-to, but my experience as both the talker and the talkee in a lecture format told me that the impact would have lasted until the moment we had some distance between us. Of course, I could have just ignored the whole thing and held my tongue until they were no longer my problem. But I didn't.

I believe their remorse was real, and I was telling the truth when I accepted their apologies. I only asked that they think twice before repeating their offensive behavior in the future. They agreed.

Tiki Trouble

Sometimes just a few letters and numbers that get transposed can change the trajectory of your whole day.

I was driving when I got a notification from the Uber app that I had a ride request, so I could only spare a glance at my phone. The address was nine hundred something McHenry Boulevard in Modesto, so I was sure it was the Tiki Lounge, a place I had dropped off and picked up passengers many times before. I accepted the ride, and a few minutes later I was pulling into the parking lot.

I waited four or five minutes and then sent a text to the rider to see what the holdup was. As it turned out, I was at the wrong address. I was supposed to be at the Tiki Lodge, the affiliated motel next door. Drop the "un" and add a "d," and the lounge becomes a lodge.

I was pulling into the parking lot of the Tiki Lodge as she was coming out of her room. I knew immediately that I had bungled into an awkward situation. My passenger was an "escort." She was wearing a short black leather skirt and a loose-fitting top. She carried her high-heel shoes instead of wearing them. I unlocked the door, and she got in.

I started the trip in the Uber app, and there was no destination. I glanced in the mirror and asked, "Where are you headed?" The response I was hoping for was "home," after a long night of . . . escorting. Instead she handed me a scrap of paper with an address in a place called Firebaugh.

I am not a native Californian, but I thought I knew the area pretty well. But what was a Firebaugh, and more importantly, where was Firebaugh, California? I entered the address into my phone, and it reported back instantly that we would be there in about ninety minutes!

We headed south toward Firebaugh in silence, except for the music on the radio. She was busy putting on makeup, and I was sure that she knew that I knew what this trip was about. It was my passenger who finally broke the silence: "You don't have to like what I do. You just have to drive." It was a statement that did not necessarily require a response, but I decided she deserved one.

I weighed my words carefully. "I don't really know anything about you, but I'm sorry that you have to do what you do to make a living."

No response.

Quite often, when I am driving people from place to place, I want to stop the car and turn to my passenger(s) and ask, What the heck is going on here? What just happened, or who are you, or what are we doing here, or what was that all about? Instead, I usually force down the questions, bite my tongue, and just keep on driving. But once in a while I get brave.

I fanned the embers of the conversation with a question—"You don't have to answer this, but how did you wind up in the escort business?" She was not thrown by the question at all. She had a very short testimonial, but her story broke my heart.

She explained that her mother had been a "hooker" on the streets of Modesto when she was a little girl. She had watched as a parade of men marched through her mother's life, but she made no mention of a father. She said that it was her mother who arranged her first "tricks" with men and that she never really thought of doing anything else.

I glanced in the mirror again and she had a look on her face that was asking, "So what do you think of me now?"

All I could come up with was, "That's a very sad story. But thank you for telling it to me."

Her response was simple: "It is what it is."

As it turns out, we were headed nowhere near the actual town of Firebaugh. The destination was one of those exits along Interstate 5, out in the middle of nowhere with two or three gas stations, a small selection of fast food and a motel. I supposed that Firebaugh was the closest town, so the travelers' "oasis" claimed the zip code.

We pulled into the motel parking lot, and she directed me to "wait over there," pointing to some spaces in the shade of a tree.

"Wait for you?"

I had not even considered that as a possibility. I was expecting to drop her off and then to take an expensive, passenger-less but solitary drive back to Modesto.

I voiced my objections: "I can't really wait around here. I need to get back to Modesto. There's not much money to be made by waiting around."

She looked at me like I was an idiot. "Do you think any Uber driver is going to come all the way out here to freakin' Fireball if you leave?"

She was right. I was stuck. "And besides," she added, "I will be back in twenty minutes."

I will spare you any details of the agony of that wait, or of the dark places my mind went, but twelve minutes later, we were back on I-5 heading north.

We hardly said a word to each other on the drive home. She was on the phone most of the trip, arranging "dates" for later in the day, comforting a friend who had been beaten up by a boyfriend, chatting with coworkers. I was alone with my thoughts—troubling thoughts.

How should I feel about this experience? On one hand, it was a lucrative trip, and if I hadn't accepted the ride, chances are the next driver would have. On the other hand, I had delivered a prostitute to her customer and waited in the shade for her.

Should I have taken a hard line and ended the ride as soon as I recognized what it was about? Should I have made an excuse—"I'm having car trouble, and I don't think I should try to drive that far"?

The truth is, quite a bit about driving for Uber bothered me. Most people use the service to avoid driving drunk, which meant, at least in part, that I was enabling my passengers to drink more. It was a conundrum.

If you are hoping to find a neat little answer to the dilemma at the end of this story, you are going to be disappointed. I struggled regularly about where my responsibility started and ended.

Uber 911

On one of the occasions when I intentionally spent the day driving in San Francisco, I got a ride request from someone at the University of California, San Francisco Medical Center emergency room. That didn't strike me as unusual. I figured I would be picking up an employee for a ride home, or maybe someone who was visiting a family member or friend. And I thought including the emergency room in the location was brilliant because the UCSF facility is huge, and finding someone among the throngs of people going in and out of the buildings is a challenge. There was no place to park on the street, and the patient drop-off and pick-up circle was jammed with cars, so I just kept cruising back and forth past the emergency entrance, hoping my passenger would eventually spot me.

The first indication that this was not going to be a typical ride came when a man wearing bright blue scrubs stepped into the street and flagged me down. I lowered my window and he asked, "Are you an Uber driver?"

"I am," I said. "Are you my passenger?"

He said, "No, but we've been waiting for you."

To my great surprise, he motioned me toward the ambulance entrance under the big red-and-white sign that said "EMERGENCY."

All of my instincts were telling me not to drive under that clearly marked "Ambulance Entrance Only" sign, but there was my guy in the scrubs, emphatically motioning for me to follow him.

It was like entering a tunnel. Once I did, I could see that there were ten or twelve parking spaces inside, but they were all marked "Ambulance Parking Only."

I started to feel the first twinges of fear when Scrubs Guy directed me to pull into one of the restricted parking spots. I had no idea what was going on. Should I get out of the car and ask what was happening? Should I throw the car into reverse and flee the scene? I opted to wait and see what would happen.

A few moments later, the automatic doors leading into the emergency room opened, and Scrubs Guy came out pushing an elderly woman in a wheelchair. Either she was very petite, or the wheelchair was impossibly large. She was clutching a purse on her lap, and her chin was on her chest.

They were heading in my direction, but I was certain that they would make a turn, or continue past me. But they didn't. He pushed her right up to my rear passenger door. My face suddenly felt hot as I came to the realization that he intended to load this frail little woman into my car.

I must have been in shock, because I didn't do or say anything. I didn't get out and open the door. I didn't help get the woman out of the wheelchair and into my back seat. I didn't ask any questions. I just sat there and watched as the man in blue scrubs transferred the woman into the seat and got her buckled in. He said "Goodbye" and shut the door, and he was gone.

The silence was deafening as she looked at me and I looked at her. I managed a weak "Hello," and she managed a weak smile.

"My name is Steve," I told her.

"Pleased to meet you" was all she said in return.

With the formalities out of the way, I was anxious to push the Start Trip button and get moving.

I pushed the button, expecting a local address, or at the most, a cross-town trip, but when the map came up on the screen, the destination was Santa Rosa! Santa Rosa is forty-five miles north of San Francisco, and our route would take us through the busy streets of San Francisco, across the Golden Gate Bridge, and up Highway 101. I could not believe what was happening. I was about to head out on a road trip with a woman who had just checked out of the ER—and I didn't even have a first aid card.

The Uber app has a feature that allows the driver and the person who arranged the ride to text or talk on the phone to each other. It's there in case you are having trouble finding each other. My phone rang, and a voice on the other end said, "I see you've picked up my mom." And for the second time in five minutes, I was stunned into silence.

She said hello a few times, and I finally responded with a question: "What is going on?" Actually it was a string of questions: "Is your mother well enough to travel? Why was she in the emergency room? Am I really taking her to Santa Rosa? Are you high?" I didn't really ask that last question, but I was thinking it very loudly.

My passenger's daughter spent the next five minutes or so answering all my questions and explaining the situation. Her mom had fainted, the paramedics were called in, her blood pressure was dangerously low, and she was rushed to the hospital in San Francisco. She had been in the ER for eighteen hours, and after a battery of tests, the doctors had determined that she was dehydrated.

The really crazy part of the story was that my passenger's daughter lived and worked in San Francisco, but for some reason she had made the call to have an Uber driver get her mother home to Santa Rosa. Maybe she was a brain surgeon or something and was right in the middle of an operation.

I was in no position to refuse the trip, since the passenger was already in my car, so I backed out of my "ambulance only" parking space and headed north.

Under normal circumstances, the drive from San Francisco to Santa Rosa is very pleasant. It was a beautiful day, and crossing the Golden Gate Bridge is always a treat. The 101 freeway winds through rolling hills dotted with vineyards and farms. But I was preoccupied with the person in the back seat. Every few seconds, I would glance in the rearview mirror, which I had adjusted down to keep checking whether she was still alive. I tried to talk to her, but she was having trouble hearing me, so I just drove.

About ten or fifteen minutes into the trip, I glanced in the mirror, and her head was tilted back and her mouth was open. I was sure she had expired in the back seat. I said "Ma'am" a little bit too emphatically, and she jerked awake. "I was just checking to see if you were doing all right," I lied. I started praying a short but urgent prayer: "Please don't let her die, Lord. Keep her alive until Santa Rosa. Don't let her die in my car."

The Uber app had us exit the freeway, and we made our way to her home. It appeared to be a luxury apartment building in the downtown area of Santa Rosa. My next dilemma was what to do with her now that we were at her destination.

I double-parked in front of the entrance and told my passenger that I would be right back. I got out and was relieved to find a woman at a desk just inside. "I'm dropping off one of your building occupants from the UCSF emergency room." I expected her to jump up and come to her tenant's aid or at least make a phone call summoning some help. But apparently the rental agreement did not include simple compassion. She just sat there.

"Can I bring my passenger inside?" I asked the unhelpful woman at the desk.

"You can bring her inside, but only as far as the elevator."

"I don't think you are understanding what I'm telling you," I shot back. "About an hour ago this lady was in a wheelchair in the emergency room of a hospital. I don't even know if she can walk."

I asked if there was someone who could help her up to her apartment and maybe check on her. There wasn't. So I went back to my car, helped my passenger out of the back seat, and had her hold on to my arm as we slowly made our way into the building. She said she would be fine as she pushed the elevator call button. When the doors opened, I got her to the back where she could hold the handrail, and pushed the button that would deliver her to her floor. And she was gone.

On the drive back toward San Francisco, I was feeling a bunch of things, but mainly I was feeling angry. I was angry that a hospital would turn a patient over to an Uber driver. I didn't sign anything or show any identification.

I was a little peeved at the lady at the apartment complex's front desk for not offering even the simplest of help, and I was especially angry at my passenger's daughter for putting her mother into a total stranger's car for a forty-five-mile trip after eighteen hours in the ER. Unless the daughter's job was a matter of national security, I could not fathom how she could not get away to drive her mother home, or at least get another member of the family or a family friend to drive her.

But most of all, I was upset with myself for going along with the plan. There were several points where I could have asked what people were thinking and if using Uber was the best idea. Instead, I went along with the scheme and made my fare. But I vowed to never let anything like that happen again.

The Bible teaches that God has a very soft spot in his heart for the vulnerable and the oppressed, for the helpless and the poor. One of the most penetrating verses in all of Scripture is in James, chapter 1. James is exhorting those who "consider themselves religious" to actually live it, emphasizing that in part, "religion that God our Father accepts as pure and faultless is this: to look after orphans and widows in their distress" (James 1:26–27).

It might be helpful to remember that if we live that long, all of us will be old someday, and some sooner than others.

Wedding Wine

Late one night, I arrived at a farm about fifteen miles east of Modesto and found six wedding guests in their twenties trying to pack themselves into a Subaru Forrester, which was only designed to carry four passengers plus the driver. Had they been successful in overcoming the Uber driver's protests regarding an illegally overloaded car and the physical space limitations, I would have had nothing to show for my trouble aside from a late night drive to the country.

I had a short conversation with my fellow Uber driver, and he gladly turned the two passengers who were outside his car over to me. We agreed that I would follow him to the group's destination, a motel along Highway 99 back in Modesto. The young man and woman who would be my traveling companions for the next thirty minutes or so climbed into my car, and we headed for town.

I introduced myself and asked how the wedding was. The guy, who was sitting up front with me, was somewhere between sloppy drunk and severely impaired. He ignored my question and went right into an explanation of the "history" that he and the young woman in the back seat had, including details that I neither needed nor wanted to hear. Of course, she vigorously denied everything he was claiming as I vigorously tried to change the subject.

"Was the wedding ceremony outside, or inside the barn?" I asked.

His response was more vulgarity, and hers was more denial from the back seat.

I tried again to steer the conversation back toward civility. "How do you two know the bride or the groom?"

He continued to spew unsolicited details, and she was now in tears.

I decided to play a card that has not failed to this day: the Jesus card.

I waited for a break in his drunken rant and said, "You know, one of the things I miss about being a minister is the weddings. I love the celebration and the joy of seeing a couple married and having a small part in it."

I looked over at him, and the expression on his face was that of a freshly lobotomized mental patient.

"What do you mean a minister?" he stammered. "Like of a church?"

I ignored him and went on: "You may or may not know this, but Jesus performed His first miracle at a wedding. The caterers had run out of wine, which would have been very embarrassing for the couple and their families. So Jesus' mother asked Him to do something. He was reluctant to get involved, because He wasn't ready to reveal that He was someone special quite yet. But He went ahead and turned some big clay pots filled with water into wine!"

I explained that Jesus probably did it because He was enjoying the celebration and didn't want to see it stop just because someone had misjudged the amount of wine to have on hand.

The mood in the car had completely changed. My young impaired friend explained to me that his brother had recently found Jesus and had been sober for several months. His dad, in response to his brother's situation, had returned to his roots in the church and was constantly talking about Jesus.

"What the heck is all this stuff about Jesus?" he demanded to know—except he didn't use anything as mild as "heck."

He might as well have handed me an engraved invitation to tell him about Jesus . . . so I did. I took him to several key verses in the book of Romans that explain the problem of sin and the solution God provided through the death of Jesus on the cross. He listened attentively, and I gave him some time to absorb the enormity of what he had just heard.

The rest of the trip into town was quiet and uneventful, except for a couple of stops for a passenger to throw up in the ditch (thankfully from the back seat of the Subaru). By the time we arrived at the motel, the young man had turned from a vulgar, arrogant jerk into a tearful and repentant child.

He apologized to the young woman in the back seat, who mouthed the words "thank you" in the rearview mirror, and to me for being obnoxious. I told him that no apology was necessary for me, but that he should sit down and talk with his brother and with his dad when he was sober and find out from them what this Jesus stuff is all about.

I hope he did.

Hail, Hail the [Deleted Expletive] Gang's All Here

It began like any normal Uber ride. I received a request to pick up a young woman in Ceres, and she let me know that we would be picking up three more passengers, all at different locations. She elected to give me turn-by-turn directions, and we headed off toward Modesto.

I talked with another Uber driver once who had established what he called "no drive" zones for himself. In other words, he had decided in advance that there were certain areas of town where he would not do business. Either he had some bad experience in that particular part of town, or he was trying to avoid potential problems. So when the request came to pick up a rider from a place he was not willing to go, the driver did not accept, and when he recognized that he was entering a "no drive" zone, he would cancel the ride. Both practices are hard on a driver's ratings, but we do what we need to do to feel safe.

As we headed into the third west-Modesto neighborhood to pick up the last passenger, I was thinking that my policy to go like a sheep wherever the Uber app or the passenger requested might need some rethinking. I needed some "no-drive" zones of my own.

We pulled up to the last house, right behind a huge vehicle that I mistook for a Modesto SWAT unit. "That can't be a good sign." I had intended to only think that thought, but then one of the guys answered my concern with "Oh, that's just the City of Modesto's Video Surveillance Unit. Some bad [expletive deleted] has been goin' down on this street."

The truck looked like an oversized armored car, and there were little windows all around the sides and back with thick, probably bulletproof glass. Under one of the side windows it said, "Smile—You Are On Video!"

"Are there people inside running the cameras?" I inquired.

"No. It's some [expletive deleted] remote control [multiple expletives deleted]."

One of the passengers had gone up to the house to get the last rider. He came out of the house pushing my fourth passenger in a wheelchair. They explained that he had gotten himself all [expletive deleted] in a drive-by shooting that had taken place in Oakland several weeks before, but that he was expected to make an almost-full recovery and would probably walk again.

Wanting to be a good Uber driver, I popped the trunk and jumped out to help fold up the wheelchair and stow it away. As I got out of the car, I realized that I had probably just become an extra in a movie about the gang problems in west Modesto. I immediately felt sick to my stomach.

The guy helping me with the wheelchair noticed that all the color had drained from my face and said, in an attempt to reassure me, "Ain't nobody gonna come after you Uberman. Ain't nobody know who you are." I honestly appreciated his pep talk, but my thought (and I actually only thought it this time) was "They may not know who I am, but I'm driving a carload of gang members around town, and I'm parked behind a [expletive deleted] Police Video Surveillance Unit!"

As we headed to the drop-off location, a party across town, the rap music was blaring and the air was blue with deleted expletives. I was planning to just drive and get the ride over as quickly as possible, but the guy up front with me had a question: "What is a white guy doing in this neighborhood after dark with a carload of people like us?"

"I believe in equal ride sharing for all," I mumbled.

He just chuckled. I knew that he knew it was equal parts lack of forethought and stupidity that had propelled me into the situation I was in.

"You're all right, Uberman," he said.

We got to the party and I helped reassemble the wheelchair, and I was free to go. I had driven about six blocks and my pulse was returning to normal when my phone rang. It was the girl from Ceres who had set the whole thing in motion. She just said, "I left my weed in your car."

I slammed on the brakes and came to a dead stop in the middle of the street. I grabbed the flashlight that I used to find house numbers in the dark and did a quick search of the back seat area. There it was. A small semimetallic packet that reminded me of what computer memory upgrade modules come in. But this packet had a sticker on it that said "Blue

Dream" and a little ball of what looked like dryer lint inside. "Got it," I said too loudly into the phone.

I told the owner of the cannabis, "You need to be outside the house, in the driveway when I get there, or I will keep on driving."

I was careful to come to a complete stop at every intersection and to drive the speed limit as I contemplated adding possession with intent to deliver to my minor roll in the gangbanger documentary.

When I pulled up, she was in the driveway. I handed her the packet, fully expecting floodlights and sirens . . . but she said "thanks," and I drove away.

I almost packed it in for the evening but decided things could only get better. I was right. The rest of the evening was, for the most part, uneventful. One person did ask if anything exciting ever happened. I just smiled into the darkness and said, "No, not really."

CHAPTER 3

Heart Inspection

THE WORD "EXAMINATION" CAN STRIKE fear in the heart of most people. It might be a test that determines a grade, or whether you get the job or not. It might be a medical exam that reveals a hidden condition. Or it might be an inspection to see if your car is Uber-worthy.

When you sign up to be an Uber driver, they dig pretty deeply down into your personal information and history. You can't just download an app and jump in the car and start driving. They require a full inquiry into a potential driver's criminal history, financial past, and driving record. They even check the sexual predator registry in all fifty states. I am happy to say that I passed all those examinations without any problem.

One of the most important examinations that Uber requires before a person begins to drive is an inspection of the car that the driver intends to use. To be a basic Uber-X vehicle, the car must be (at this writing) a 2009 or newer, non-salvage title, four-door sedan with seats and seat belts to accommodate four passengers and the driver.

In addition to those basic requirements, the car must undergo a fairly rigorous annual safety inspection performed by a certified mechanic. He or she works from a checklist provided by Uber and takes a look at about forty items on a potential Uber car. Tire tread depth, brake pad thickness, all lights, horn, and so on. There are also items on the list that mean nothing to me—tie rods, bushings, ball joints. I don't know what they are, but I do know I have them.

One day when I was getting ready to go out Ubering, I switched on the Uber app and it shut itself off. A page opened automatically and informed me that my vehicle inspection form had expired and I could not Uber until the problem was corrected.

WHAAAAAT! How could something so debilitating happen without any warning? No email, no text message, no calls or voicemails. I was dead in the water late on a Thursday afternoon with a car that could not be driven for Uber.

I did a little investigation and discovered the problem. I use Gmail as my email server and it has a (mostly) handy feature that autosorts incoming mail into three categories.

The three classifications of mail are Primary, the important stuff like personal notes and replies to things I have written to other people; Social, mostly notifications and messages generated by sites like Facebook and LinkedIn; and finally, Promotions, a nice way of saying junk mail.

I did a search of my whole computer and discovered that Uber had in fact been trying to warn me that my inspection certificate was about to expire. They had sent three separate notes telling me to get off my butt and get the car to a mechanic. But for some reason, the warnings were going into the "Promotions" mailbox and not the "Primary" one. So the news that my car was about to become undrivable was among the discount Viagra ads and coupons for 20 percent off at Chili's.

The next morning, I was at the garage when the doors opened at 8:00 a.m., form in hand. I turned over the car to an employee and headed for the lobby, which occupied about fifty-seven square feet. I felt like an anxious family member waiting for the doctor to come out of surgery and deliver a report. "Everything went fine" or "We did everything we could. I'm so sorry for your loss." My Toyota Camry had 264,000 miles on it at the time, and honestly, I was hoping for the best but prepared for bad news. I would have paced, but there were only four square feet of paceable floor in the waiting area and pacing outside the unisex bathroom seemed like a bad idea.

Finally, the mechanic, covered to his elbows in grease, came into the waiting area and called not my name but the car year and model: "2005 Toyota Camry."

I took that as a bad sign. I rose slowly and approached him.

"I found just one issue," he said, devoid of emotion.

I assumed the worst, "Was it the transmission?" I asked. "Or the engine or the tie rods, or some other hidden 'issue'?"

He held up a lightbulb about the size of a pencil eraser and said. "This has gotta be replaced before I can sign off on your car to return to service."

"How much will that cost?" I asked.

"Five dollars—installed."

I ignored the fact that I could have purchased the same bulb at Walmart for eighty-nine cents.

I wanted to turn to the other people in the undersized waiting area and shout, "She's going to live! She's going to make it!" but instead I pulled a five-dollar bill from my wallet and handed it to the grease-covered mechanic. He put it into his cash drawer and headed back into the shop.

I am pleased to report that I went right home, scanned the form, and emailed it to Uber. There was a notice that it might take up to forty-eight hours to process the form, but by 4:00 p.m., the inspection was approved, and I was back out on the road, picking up and dropping off riders and collecting material for this book.

As I was driving around that evening, I had the thought that regular examinations are a good idea for people as well as cars, even though they can be equally scary and expensive. Taking an honest look at what is going on in my life should be a regular part of my routine.

I tend to be kind of lazy when it comes to taking a good, hard look at how I am doing. If something is seriously out of kilter, like if an important relationship is broken or if I'm having trouble shaking a bout of depression, I get right on that.

But I tend to let the little things accumulate. My Bible reading gets overlooked a few times or Barb and I are not spending enough time together. Those things get pushed to the side, and the little pile of problems grows into a big pile.

The Apostle Paul, in his letter to the church at Corinth, suggests that a good time for spiritual self-examination is when we gather around the table as a family to celebrate communion. He writes, "Everyone ought to examine themselves before they eat of the bread and drink from the cup" (2 Corinthians 11:28a). It's a good time to remember what Jesus did at the cross, and an appropriate time to do a little inspection of our own lives.

Maybe I am harboring some anger against someone or feeling jealous because my car is not as nice as the one I parked next to in the church parking lot.

I need to be regularly inspecting my life and making corrections and adjustments along the way. If I'm not, then I should not be surprised one day to have a wheel fall off, or to hear scary noises from under the hood, or have the tie rods . . . come untied.

$10,000 Hamburger

I have been pretty frustrated after spending the better part of a day at the Department of Motor Vehicles, especially after standing in the wrong line and being forced to start my wait over. It can be a maddening place, but I had never seen anyone in actual tears coming out of the DMV.

The woman in tears was following a man that I later found out was her husband. He had called for an Uber to take them home. He climbed in the front, and she got in the back, continuing to sob. "How are you doing?" I asked, even though I was pretty sure they were not doing well.

"I've just had the worst week of my life," he reported.

The man spoke for both of them as their story spilled out.

They were from Tracy, a town about forty minutes northwest of where I live. Their story began at a party on the previous weekend at a friend's house in Modesto.

He said, "It wasn't a 'wild' kind of party with a live rock band and guns being fired into the air. It wasn't even the kind of party that would eventually force a neighbor to call the police. It was a family birthday party. There were kids and games, a barbeque, and some beer."

A small twinge in my stomach that told me that "some beer" was going to become a major part of this story.

At some point in the afternoon, my front-seat passenger decided that he was hungry. He knew that there was a McDonald's less than a mile from the party that wouldn't require any freeway driving or even taking a busy street. And even though he had taken a bite out of a six-pack of beer, he got behind the wheel of his pickup and headed out in search of a Quarter Pounder with Cheese.

"I don't know what I did to attract the attention of the police officer," he wondered aloud. "Maybe I was swerving a little or driving too slowly or too fast. I was being super careful, but maybe I forgot to signal for a turn. I don't know, but for whatever reason, I was sitting in my truck with a cop behind me and the feeling that I was going to be sick." His story was punctuated by a loud sob from the back seat.

The officer did a field sobriety test and, based on that, had my unfortunate friend blow into a breathalyzer. Being a smart reader, I'm sure you have figured the outcome of the test. He was charged with driving under the influence of alcohol.

He spent nearly all of the ride home listing the consequences he was now facing because of his decision to drive drunk. His car was impounded and would be stored at a police impound lot for a month, which would cost him about $2,700. (*Sob.*) His driver's license was suspended, which is a big deal for most people, but for him it was a *huge* deal because his job was installing and servicing package-handling equipment all over northern California, which required a commercial driver's license, without which he might lose his job and income. (*Loud sob.*) He was arrested, booked, and put in jail overnight, which he said was easily the most humiliating and terrifying thing that had ever happened to him.

His wife had to make arrangements to post bail and he would be required to appear in court before a judge, which would necessitate hiring an attorney. There would be fines, possible jail time or probation, and mandatory driving school that he would have to pay for, and best case, his auto insurance premiums would rise sharply or worst case, his policy would be canceled. (*Weeping and gnashing of teeth from the rear seat.*)

He said that the attorney he had hired had told him that the total cost (not counting the possible loss of his income) would probably be somewhere between $10,000 and $18,000. All I could manage was "Yikes!" which may have been the greatest understatement of my life to that point.

After I dropped them off and headed for home, I had the opportunity to contemplate the obvious lesson of my passenger's experience: driving drunk can get you in all kinds of trouble. But as I thought about the consequences faced by my passenger, I was convinced that there was a more universal, personal lesson in this story.

I spend a large part of my day making decisions. Most of them are small and relatively inconsequential—like the decision to let another driver pull out from a parking lot in front of me, or choosing to be honest, even when no one would know the difference. But the thing about decisions is that they slowly become habits—our decisions become our default reactions.

If every choice we made had an immediate consequence like a DUI and the prospect of a huge financial hit, we would all be a lot more careful. But choices tend to pile up slowly over time, like a faucet dripping into a bucket. The process seems impossibly slow, but given enough time, the bucket fills, with no room for anything else.

I decided on the way back home that I would be more intentional about the decisions I made and that I would try to identify the decisions that had become habits and evaluate whether they were habits worth keeping or breaking. And I decided that if I were ever at a party and got the munchies, I would just make a peanut butter and jelly sandwich.

The Purse of Great Price

Online auctions have become a part of our American cultural fabric. The original digital marketplace was the brainstorm of a computer programmer named Pierre Omidyar, who launched eBay from his San Jose living room in September of 1995. The first item to sell on the site was a broken laser pointer for $14.83. In 2015, an estimated 17.94 billion dollars in business was conducted by eBay. That's a bunch of broken laser pointers!

Around the same time eBay was born, a newcomer to the San Francisco Bay area named Craig Newmark decided to start an online listing of concerts and events as a way to get to know people. The idea caught on quickly, and soon people were networking their resumes and reviewing restaurants and selling their stuff to each other. Remarkably, after all these years, Craigslist has remained nearly commercial free, except for a very small number of listings that come with a fee, like posting a job opening in multiple cities or renting an apartment. Craigslist is kind of like a global garage sale without the hassle of finding a place to park.

I got a ride request one evening from a young woman who had sold a purse on Craigslist to a person in Lodi, California, a city about forty-five miles up scenic Highway 99. Lodi was made famous by Credence Clearwater Revival in their 1969 song "Lodi." The song contains the lyric "Oh Lord, stuck in Lodi again."

I did a little research and learned that the band was often stuck in Lodi (and other small northern California towns) because their bar tab would exceed their earnings for a gig at the local club or tavern. That's all I have to say about that.

I found the purse lady's house without any trouble. Once there, I learned that her boyfriend would be joining us for the trip, which was fine with me, until he asked if he might be allowed to take control of the radio. In my 2005 Toyota Camry, that literally meant choosing the radio station and setting the volume. The car predated those fancy USB inputs and Bluetooth gizmos.

Unfortunately, the boyfriend was a big fan of gangster rap, and in no time at all, we were thumping our way north toward Lodi.

The prearranged meeting place was a RiteAid drugstore in a residential part of Lodi, and we found it easily. The timing of our arrival was perfect, as the buyer pulled in at almost the same moment. The seller of the purse, which I never got a look at because it was in a shopping bag, and the potential buyer approached each other cautiously.

MC Obnoxious and I stayed in the car and continued to listen to his profanity-laced rap songs. By this time, I would have gladly capped his . . . well, let's just say the music was getting on my nerves.

The deal was made quickly, and my passenger got back in the car with a fistful of cash. She told her boyfriend that she had sold the purse for $100, a price that, I gathered from the broad smile on her face, she was very satisfied with. We headed back toward Modesto and the prospect of my regaining control of the radio.

The Uber driver application is not like a meter in a taxi. There is no running total for the fare as the ride progresses. The cost of the trip is only calculated when the trip is over— and the trip was over. I dropped them off where I had picked them up, said thank you and good night, and slid the slider on my iPhone to end the ride.

When the total fare appeared on my screen (and I am not making this up), it said $99.76! I was never very good at math, but anyone could see that her net profit for the sale of the purse, even if she received it as a gift or found it in a parking lot, was $0.24.

I knew that she and her boyfriend would be receiving the same report that I was reading at that very moment, so I pressed the accelerator down hard to put some distance between myself and the possibility of an awkward situation.

She had a good plan: sell her item on Craigslist, where there is no fee or commission or shipping charges, meet the buyer in a public place like a well-lit parking lot to avoid the risk of getting robbed, and take the boyfriend along in case things go sideways. The only variable she had failed to calculate properly was my part: the cost of transportation, which had eaten up all her profit except for $0.24.

As I reflected on what became known in my mind as "The Purse of Great Price" incident, I remembered a season in the ministry of Jesus when He was wildly popular. He was followed by huge crowds wherever He went. He was like a rock star.

People were drawn in by His miracles and the possibility of free meals. And Jesus would have none of it. He preached a sermon with some difficult teaching about the costs of discipleship—hardship and sacrifice, loneliness and cross bearing.

And then He told two very short stories: The first was about a man who wanted to build a tower but failed to consider the cost and ran out of funds before the project was complete. The tower would stand as a monument to his failure to plan properly.

The second story was about a king who got word that an invading army was approaching. A prudent king would find out how many soldiers were closing in on his territory, do a quick head count of his own army, and if badly outnumbered, send a delegation to negotiate a treaty instead of waging a war that was certain to wipe him out.

And then Jesus ended His sermon with a statement that would send people running for the exits: "In the same way, those of you who do not give up everything you have cannot be my disciples" (Luke 14:33).

Jesus is not looking to make us all rich. There are television evangelists who would have us believe that if we don't have a mansion and big white teeth and drive a Lexus, we must be doing it wrong. But the message of Jesus is simple: the cost of following is everything you have. Complete transfer of ownership. If you don't know this going in, you'll get an unpleasant surprise—much like I imagine my purse-selling passenger experienced. But unlike her, you're still getting the best deal anywhere: citizenship in the kingdom of God.

Treasure under Our Noses

Sometimes when I was feeling lazy or having a hard time getting motivated to Uber I would start my "shift" at home. All that meant was that instead of driving to my usual spot where I would wait for ride requests, I would start Ubering from the comfort of my family room. I would get everything ready to go, sit down on the couch, start the app, and wait for something to happen.

On one particular spring day, I used the start-at-home method and received a ride request within only a few minutes. The rider was in Hughson, a community located a few miles east of where I live. I arrived at the rider's house in less than five minutes. He was a thirtysomething guy dressed in what I would classify as semiwestern wear—a plaid shirt, Wrangler jeans, and cowboy boots. He hopped in the front seat, and I hit the Start Trip button. Our destination was a town I have talked about in previous chapters, Oakdale.

Oakdale is something of an enigma. It's an old town, founded in 1871, and has remained medium-small, with around twenty thousand residents. It was the home of a satellite chocolate factory for The Hershey Company, until the plant was relocated to Mexico in 2008. But as you drive into town, the "Welcome to Oakdale" sign says "The Cowboy Capital of the World."

Not "The Cowboy Capital of Stanislaus County" or "the Central Valley" or "Northern California"— the world!

I could not help but assume that this was a self-designation. I think there are other towns in this area that would take exception to Oakdale's claim. Like Vacaville, for instance, whose name literally means "cow town," or Stockton, whose name also literally means "cow town." Everyone who was watching television in the 1960s and early 1970s knew that the Cartwright boys would make the trip down from the Ponderosa Ranch on the shores of Lake Tahoe to Stockton to go all cowboy.

"Are you going to stay in Oakdale and work the whole night?" my passenger asked.

I gave him a look that said, "Why would I want to do that?" And he shot back an expression that asked if I had just arrived from another planet.

He said, "The rodeo, man! The rodeo."

It turns out that every year, on the second weekend in April, the Oakdale Saddle Club hosts a three-day event that includes the selection of a rodeo queen, a rodeo dance, a rodeo parade, team roping, barrel racing, and on Sunday, a cowboy church service.

The main event is a full-blown demonstration rodeo sanctioned by the Professional Rodeo Cowboy Association (PRCA). The PRCA is the largest rodeo organization in the world and holds events in the United States, Canada, Mexico, and Brazil, with members from all around the world. Its championship event is the National Finals Rodeo held in Las Vegas in December. I had no idea the Oakdale Rodeo was going on twenty minutes from my house.

My passenger was meeting his wife at the H-B Saloon (pronounced "H Bar B Saloon"), and as we approached the downtown area, traffic became very heavy. I could only get him close to the H-B, due to the large crowd, spilling out into the street. Close must have been good enough, because he wished me luck and jumped out of the car.

When I ended the ride, the map that appeared on my phone was completely orange and red, which meant that Oakdale was experiencing a "surge." In other words, there were more people who needed a ride than there were available Uber drivers, and the price of a ride would increase accordingly.

I had experienced a surge a few times before, but the surge was usually in a different place than I was, and by the time I arrived on the scene, a bunch of other drivers had shown up too, and the surge was over. But I was right in the middle of this one, and for the time being, it was going to be a good night.

I started accepting ride requests, which were almost all short trips between locations around Oakdale. Normally, these quick hops would only have been worth about four dollars, but because of the surge, they were three and four times that. It was a blur of pickups and drop-offs that did not seem to be slowing down.

The one trip I made out of town was for an unfortunate party of four who had dinner reservations in Modesto and had to pay over forty dollars for a one-way trip because their ride originated in Oakdale. I dropped them off and ignored any local requests so that I could rejoin the chaos created by the rodeo.

As the evening progressed, the effect of people's alcohol consumption began to have an impact. I had a couple try to get into my car at a stoplight while I was on my way to pick up someone else because they saw my Uber and Lyft stickers in the windshield. I witnessed either a low-speed chase or simply a police officer following an intoxicated cowboy on a horse so he wouldn't get rear-ended.

One of the most memorable events of the evening occurred when a couple in the back seat disappeared from my rearview mirror and I realized they were attempting to have . . . carnal relations in my car. I yelled for them to sit up, separate, and buckle their seat belts or I was going to put them out on the street right where we were.

As the time for the main rodeo event approached, I got a call from a group of four who needed a ride from their hotel to the rodeo grounds. I picked them up and headed for the entrance. What I had not heard was that due to the rain on the previous night, the parking lot was mostly mud, and only four-wheel-drive vehicles should attempt to enter.

I pulled into the lot and immediately started bogging down in the thick muck. I knew that if I stopped, we would be stuck, so I kept my foot on the accelerator and tried to head for the exit. At one point, we drove over something solid—probably a cement parking stop—and my passengers screamed and bounced up near the roof of the car. We slipped and slid until we got back on solid ground. I dropped the passengers at a gas station next to the rodeo grounds and told them they would need to walk to the stadium. One of the men in the group gave me a five-dollar bill and said he had enjoyed the ride.

I broke my own rule that night and continued to drive until the requests for rides slowed to a trickle around 2:30 a.m. It was an exhausting evening, but my Uber app reported that I had made just over $350!

On the way home, I realized that I had stumbled into the Oakdale Rodeo because I had started my app at home instead of on the way to Modesto, and as result, I had discovered a lucrative opportunity right under my nose.

The experience made me wonder how much I miss in life because I'm just not paying attention. Maybe there is someone I see every day who has an incredible story to tell, but I haven't taken the time to listen to it. Maybe there is someone I think I know who has a hidden talent that would give me chills if I would just get to know them and discover it. I may have some family heirloom that is collecting dust in my attic that is worth a fortune—right under my nose.

I put a note in my calendar on the second weekend in April so I wouldn't miss the next year. It read "Uber in Oakdale—The Cowboy Capital of the World."

For God So Loved the World

My basic understanding concerning how God feels about us changed dramatically when we had kids. I'm not saying my understanding is more complete or better than anyone else's. It's just that my definition of love and what love looks like was completely reshaped when Barb and I made room for children in our lives.

I understood that love disciplines, because we wanted our boys to grow up knowing about right and wrong. I learned that the formerly incomprehensible statement "This hurts me more than it hurts you" is actually true!

When our kids were hurt or suffering physically or emotionally, I actually prayed that God would somehow transfer the pain to me so that they would be free of it. (I tried the Vulcan mind meld once, but I was unsuccessful.) I understood that I could be disappointed in my kids but love them just as much as I did before the disappointment.

And I believe I would give my life to protect my family, though I thankfully haven't had to test this conviction. Granted, my love for my children is merely a reflection of how God loves us, but life in the laboratory of reality has, no doubt, pushed out the edges of my understanding.

I got a late-night Uber request to pick up a passenger in a not-so-good part of Ceres. I started navigating toward the location and almost immediately received a phone call. The call was from the dad of the kid I was going to pick up—a late-teen boy who had been dropped off by his crew leader at the end of a two-day job doing inventory at some large department stores in the Sacramento area.

The father on the other end of the line made no attempt to hide his extreme sense of urgency. "I need you to get to my son as quickly as possible. You need to get him into your car and safely home."

"I'm only about ten minutes away," I assured him.

"Just get there as fast as you can," he repeated.

About five minutes later, I got another call from the dad. This time he was in an outright panic. His son had called him. He was afraid. There were suspicious looking cars in the area, and his phone battery was about to die.

He wanted to know if I could drive any faster. "This is my son!" he reminded me. He told me what his son would be wearing and that he would be waiting on the sidewalk and could I possibly hurry because this was his son.

"I have sons," I told him. "I know how you feel."

By this time I was channeling Gene Hackman in *The French Connection*. I would get there as quickly as I possibly could.

I came screeching around the corner, and my headlights lit up a kid who fit the description I had been given. He got in the front seat just as my phone rang again. I handed it to him and said, "This is going to be your dad."

He told his dad, "I'm in the car and headed for home."

I gave him a chance to settle down a bit by asking a few questions—What was his job like? Was out-of-town travel typical? Why did he get dropped off in an industrial park in Ceres so late at night? Was the company hiring? He was a polite young man and answered my questions respectfully.

When we were getting close to his house, I decided to take a chance. I said, "Your dad loves you a lot. He was pretty worked up about getting you off the street."

He was not fazed by the remark at all, and his response was great—"That's just the way he is. He worries. He wants what's best for me."

"All good dads are like that," I offered.

We arrived at his house, where his dad was waiting at the door. The son got a hug, and I got a thank-you wave and the satisfaction that I had played a very minor role in a very ordinary drama about a loving dad worrying over his son.

Later, as I was replaying what had happened, I was struck by the raw intensity of the love that this father had for his child. He was not trying to play it cool. He didn't care that I knew what he was feeling. He was unashamedly driven by love for his son.

I was surprised to feel myself getting choked up. As I thought about that dad, I sensed the same kind of love from God for me, His child. A love that feels no joy in discipline. A love that still loves me, even when I am a disappointment. A love that was willing to take my pain so I wouldn't have to experience it.

Even though our less-than-perfect attempts to love and protect our kids are just a shadow of God's perfect love, they hint at the incredible passion God has for us.

My Rambo Moments

One of my favorite movies from the '80s is the cult classic *First Blood*. It's the story of John Rambo, a Vietnam-era Special Forces veteran who gets mistreated by a local sheriff and then spends the rest of the movie blowing up the fictional town of Hope, Washington.

Near the end of the movie, Colonel Sam Trautman, played by Richard Crenna, is called in to coax Rambo (Sylvester Stallone) back from the brink. They have this remarkably insightful conversation where John Rambo explains the dichotomy between his former life in the military and his present situation as a drifter. Let's allow Rambo to explain:

For me civilian life is nothing! In the field, we had a code of honor. You watch my back, I watch yours. Back here, there's nothing! Back there, I can fly a gunship, I could drive a tank, I was in charge of million-dollar equipment. Back here, I can't even hold a job parking cars.

At this point in the movie, Rambo suffers a post-traumatic-stress-induced break and proceeds to relive the horrors of war, specifically the gruesome death of his buddy in a Saigon bar from a bomb delivered by a child.

I have very little in common with John Rambo. I am not a veteran, and although I am grateful for the service of those who are and were, I am also grateful to have never experienced the horrors of war personally. I have never been mistreated by a maniacal sheriff (played brilliantly by actor Brian Dennehy) or shot up a small town with an M-60 machine gun, and my pectoral muscles will never look like Rambo's.

I have, however, applied for a job with the City of Modesto as a parking lot attendant, which didn't yield so much as an automatic email indicating the receipt of my application . . . and I also share the vague sense of disconnect between my old life in the ministry and my new life as a "civilian."

This is going to sound like whining, but it was hard transitioning from being near the center of things in a church to living closer to the fringes. Just a few years ago, I was preaching every week. I was part of a leadership team and a trusted pastor, called on to perform the sacred duties of the office. And then seemingly overnight, I was holding out hope for the parking lot job. Okay, that not only sounded like whining—it was.

To help keep the whining to a minimum, I found some relief from the discipline of praying through the Psalms. There are two things to notice as you exercise that discipline. First, David was not shy about his complaining to God. He said in Psalm 142, "I cry aloud to the LORD; I lift up my voice to the LORD for mercy. I pour out before him my complaint; before him I tell my trouble (Psalm 142:1–2).

Now, I am not recommending a campaign of complaint against God, especially if your complaining tends toward the grumbling side of the spectrum. But God seems able to handle our carefully chosen complaints. In fact, He may even enjoy hearing them from time to time.

The second thing I notice is that David's complaints always lead back to a place of hope. The complaining works its way around to faith and confidence and worship. Psalm 142 ends this way: "Set me free from my prison that I may praise your name. Then the righteous will gather about me because of your goodness to me" (Psalm 142:7 NIV).

I admit it. I have my John Rambo moments, when life seems unfair and circumstances seem to pile up around me and threaten to overwhelm. I would guess that if you came into my office—if I had an office—and were honest, you'd admit to those moments too. But when I stop and recall the past faithfulness of God, or He gently reminds me that He is good, or He whacks me on the side of the head, I eventually make it back to a place of hope. I can agree with the Psalmist—"From the LORD comes deliverance" (Psalm 3:8).

Escorts, Pizza Guys, and Uber Drivers

A WISE PERSON ONCE SAID, "THERE are two kinds of people in the world: The ones who put people into categories, and the ones who don't."

When people got into my car for an Uber ride, they usually fit neatly into one of several categories. I didn't keep statistics, and there was nothing scientific about my observations. I just enjoyed talking to people and finding out what made them tick.

The first, and most common, type of rider exuded a "don't talk to me" vibe from the back seat, passenger side. I would always ask how people were doing and usually a second question to see if I could strike up a conversation. "I'm not a fan of these temperatures in the hundreds. What about you?"

If the passenger didn't want to talk, they made it clear. They checked their text messages, or pulled their hoodie up over their head, or put in their earbuds, or avoided eye contact in the rearview mirror. I suppose they just wanted to get where they were going without the inconvenience of a conversation. I would say that somewhere between a third and half of passengers in the greater Modesto area fell into this category.

The second major category of rider was the "I wasn't planning to talk to the Uber driver, but he was so good at drawing me out, I couldn't help myself" group. Getting this rider to talk required quick thinking and keen listening and observation skills.

I picked up one such young woman one afternoon, and she said something in response to my follow-up question that revealed she was not from the local area, so I asked her, "Where are you from?"

"I'm from the Portland area," she said.

"That's where I grew up, too." I glanced at her in the rearview mirror. "I still have quite a bit of family there. What part of Portland?"

"You've probably never heard of it," she said. "It's called Clackamas."

"Not only have I heard of it," I told her, "I have a sister who lives in Clackamas and I was born in Oregon City, the county seat of Clackamas County."

She laughed out loud. "I was born in Clackamas, at the Kaiser hospital."

"I know right where that is," I told her. "On Sunnyside Road, right down the street from where my mom and dad used to live."

We were off to the races! I counted it as a personal victory to convert a "don't talk to me" into a "talker."

The next type of passenger climbed into the rear seat, passenger side, with the clear hope and expectation that I would talk to them. All they needed was a little prompting, and before long, they were telling me about their car problems or new job or what they had planned for dinner on the weekend.

I enjoyed these riders immensely. I am a people person and love chatting and exchanging stories and experiences. Every person has a story to tell if you are willing to engage in conversation.

The final major rider group included the people who climbed into the front seat (which is not traditional in a taxi or limo setting) with the attitude "We are going to talk, like it or not." I admit these were my favorite passengers.

The subject matter was as varied as the people in the front seat, from politics to organic gardening. They wanted to know all about what it took to drive for Uber and the weirdest thing that had ever happened on the job (tough question). They talked about their problems and their jobs and their families and their lives. It was really a hoot, and I often hated to see their destination approach on the Uber app.

There is one more single rider category, one I never encountered personally: the person who might get into the car—probably at night—and sit in the rear seat, driver's side. *Brrrrrrrr*. The thought of it sends a cold chill up my spine. This situation is reserved for serial killers (or possibly visitors from the UK who both drive and operate a motor vehicle on the wrong side).

All of these observations pertained to single riders. Put two, three, or four passengers into the car, and the dynamics changed completely. Either they would talk among themselves and I would just listen, or I would be included in the discussion, which was a rare treat.

It's amazing to me how a job that has you around people for eight hours at a time can be so lonely. It was quite possible to go an entire shift without having a meaningful conversation with anybody.

Driving for Uber dramatically changed my attitude toward people who work in the service industry. When I am around a waiter or waitress, or a convenience store clerk, or an Uber driver, I make an effort to talk with them like they are human. I try to look them in the eye and ask them how they are and really mean it. I make a point of telling them they did a great job and that I appreciate their hard work.

When I was a pastor, I took it for granted that people valued my opinion. They would actually make an appointment to talk with me. Sometimes people would stop by my office without an appointment just to chat, and often I would resent their visits as interruptions to my busy schedule. But now if someone just drops by to see me, I will keep talking to them until my voice gives out.

More than Delivery

When he got into the car, my first impression was that he looked like Jon Heder (minus the over-sized glasses), the actor who portrayed Napoleon Dynamite in the 2004 American comedy with the same name. He wasn't, of course. He was a young man, around nineteen or twenty, who needed a ride somewhere.

He chose the back seat, which meant that it was about even money that our conversation would go much beyond "How are you doing today?" and "Fine, how about you?" But I made a run at getting the conversation started with a weak attempt at humor. "Are you headed to school or work . . . or something fun?" He got my joke and chuckled. He was headed to work, a take-and-bake pizza place located in a strip mall somewhere in Modesto.

We talked pizza for a while. "Does your place have a gluten-free crust?" I asked. "My wife is gluten-free, and we are always on the lookout for good crust."

They did, but he had never tried it.

"I have never had very much luck with take-and-bake pizza," I admitted. "They usually come out of the oven either burnt or all doughy."

"The key," he explained expertly, "is proper oven temperature and placement of the pizza as close to the middle of the oven as possible."

He asked me a few standard questions about Uber driving. How long had I been at it? Did I have another job?

The conversation moved along to his efforts to get his own car. "I put part of every paycheck in the bank so that I can quit relying on Uber for transportation."

"Are you planning to get something used or new?" I asked.

"I am actually thinking about something like what you are driving. An older Toyota Camry or Corolla."

I gave my thirty-second testimony about how our car had so far provided almost 265,000 miles of reliable service with not much more than regular oil changes and a few minor repairs, like replacing the starter and water pump.

"You are really smart to save up for the car instead of getting a loan," I commended him.

Our conversation continued at a comfortable pace. He told me that he was the oldest employee at the pizza place, besides the owner, and that the younger staff treated him with some measure of contempt and that he felt awkward around them.

I responded again with a lame try for a laugh. "I went through an awkward stage too, but that all changed when I became an Uber driver." He seemed to think that was funny . . . or maybe he was just being polite.

As the minutes ticked by, our conversation took several more turns. We talked about his home situation, his fears about what would happen to America, depending on who became president, and his lack of a five-year plan.

He was articulate and thoughtful. He struck me as an "old soul" in the body of a nineteen-year-old kid.

When we pulled up to his workplace, I ended the ride and thanked him for using Uber. I told him that it had been nice talking to him.

His response: "Thank you for talking to me."

Out of all the rides I had given that was the only time someone had thanked me for talking to them. There were appreciative comments: "Thank you for a safe trip." "Your car smells nice." "I appreciate you coming all the way out to Oakdale to pick me up." But no one had ever thanked me for talking to them. The remark seemed so loaded, so obviously a statement, that I could not resist asking him, "What do you mean?"

He paused for a few seconds, weighing his words. "It's just that sometimes I feel like a package being delivered. But you talked to me, and I appreciated it."

It made me kind of sad that he was genuinely grateful for sixteen minutes of simple conversation about take-and-bake pizza technique and used cars and what it's like to be an awkward kid in this day and age.

I put out my hand and told him that I had enjoyed talking with him too. He shook my hand and headed to work . . . and I have never seen him again.

As a pastor, I had no trouble buying into the concept that every person is loved by God and created in His image. I had been taught that principle my whole life, and to a certain extent, I really believed it. The limiting factor was the simple matter of proximity. I spent almost all my time around people who were, for the most part, just like me. We shared the same basic beliefs and a common worldview. We had similar standards of behavior, and our priorities were a lot alike.

One of the things I slowly discovered as an Uber driver was that my world was very small. There were all kinds of other people out there who I probably would have never met if I had not had problems with my health. Every ride that I gave reinforced the truth that every single person—from the prostitute to the refugee, from the business woman to the gangbanger—is loved by God and created in His image.

Like my take-and-bake pizza friend, they are not packages that need delivering. They are not cargo that needs to get from point A to point B. They are people with value. Each one has a story that is worth listening to.

So wherever I find myself, I will continue to attempt conversations with complete strangers, knowing that most will deflect my efforts and resist letting someone in. But once in a while, an actual conversation will happen, and I believe that is a very good thing.

Close Encounters of the "Escort" Kind

There are some universal principles that quickly became self-evident to Uber drivers. For instance, when people are drunk, they believe that they are funny and charming. In all but a few cases, they aren't. Another thing that most Uber drivers would agree on is that the later it gets, the weirder it gets. And closely related to that truth is this one: if the pick-up location is a motel late at night . . . nothing good will come of it.

I pulled into the Apex Motel parking lot a little before 11:00 p.m. Rita was coming down the steps at the end of the building, talking on her phone. I lowered the passenger-side window to ask her if she had requested an Uber, but she ignored me and just got in the back seat. There was no hesitation. No caution. She had done this before.

She paused her conversation just long enough to tell me to head for Stockton, about thirty-five miles north, and that she would give me an address in a few minutes. She was telling someone on the line that they could see her picture on some website and that she also had a Facebook page. When she paused again, she delivered on her promise to provide an address in Stockton. I entered it, and she asked when we should arrive.

"About forty minutes," I said.

Rita told the person on the phone that we would be there in twenty.

She ended the call, and I could hear her digging around in her purse. "Can I smoke?" she asked.

"No, sorry," I answered. "This is my private car and I don't want it to smell like cigarettes."

She muttered something that I didn't quite catch, but her tone suggested that she was not a fan of my "no smoking" policy.

"I'm Rita," she said, and continued her search for whatever she was trying to find in her purse.

"I'm Steve. Nice to meet you."

She asked a few of the usual questions, including what I did for work before, or in addition to, Ubering. I had no idea where it would take our conversation, but I gave my normal answer: "I have been a pastor for about thirty-five years."

"You've probably figured out that I'm an escort," she said without hesitation.

First of all, that's not the word I was thinking. Second, I knew we were at a pivotal point in our conversation.

She added, "You probably don't approve of what I do."

She was right; I didn't approve. But I was also fairly certain that she had a story that led her to her present circumstances. And I was also confident that her story did not include a chapter where, as a little girl, she dreamed of growing up to become an . . . "escort."

She was probably expecting a lecture, or an abrupt end to our conversation, but I decided to take a chance. Granted, most of my courage came from the fact that I would likely never see Rita again, but it still felt like a risk. I asked her a question—"Do you know much about Jesus?"

Her response was priceless—"Do you mean the Son of God . . . that Jesus?" She admitted that she didn't know much.

So I spent the next few miles trying to explain in a way that she could grasp that Jesus was a big disappointment to the church of His day because He kept spending time with people who were way out on the edges of society. He would hang out with rough-talking fishermen and sit down to eat with tax collectors and prostitutes. I went on to explain that not only did He spend time with those people—Jesus actually loved them, and they loved Him back.

I kept an eye on Rita in the back seat. She had stopped digging through her purse and seemed to be listening, but I wasn't sure if she was buying it.

I awkwardly explained that the thing that ticked off the religious leaders more than anything was probably that

Jesus seemed to like the wrong people. It was one of the main things that got Him killed.

And I told her that Jesus said if we knew Him, we knew His Father's heart, which means that God loves imperfect people . . . like prostitutes and Uber drivers.

"There's probably a Bible in your motel room somewhere," I said, "and if you want to read about it yourself, you can find a section near the back, under the name Luke. In the fifteenth chapter, there is a great story about how God has a special place in His heart for people who have wandered far away from Him."

I usually send people to the book of John when they are just starting to read the Bible, but given the circumstances, that seemed like a bad idea. I was pretty sure that prostitutes referred to their clients as generic "Johns."

I wish I could tell you that Rita broke down. Or that she cried out, "What must I do to be saved?" She didn't.

Her phone rang, and it was her client asking for a new ETA. I told her seven minutes; she told him we were just pulling onto his street.

When we finally did arrive, he was standing on the corner in a residential neighborhood. I expected her to get out, but instead, he got in. I asked where we were going, and to my surprise, she said, "Back to the motel in Modesto."

The drive back was awkwardly free of any conversation—any! All I remember is thinking of stupid questions about the ride's circumstances: *Who pays for the Uber fare? Will Rita get reimbursed, or will she write it off on her taxes?* Or, *How did a guy in Stockton get connected with an "escort" in Modesto? Is there some kind of agency or online site that arranges the details of a "date"? And what if we got pulled over right now for a burned-out taillight and the officer figured out what was going on? Would I go to jail for being the driver?* That last question haunts me to this day.

I finally dropped them off and headed for home where I told Barb the whole story.

Amazingly, a few days later, I got a ride request and recognized the name Rita. It was a weekday afternoon, and the pick-up location was a place called DD's Discounts—a low-priced variety store in our area—so I figured it would be safe.

I located Rita, shopping bags in hand. She was accompanied by a man that she introduced as her husband. She told him, "This is Steve. He is a pastor." His response was a big smile accompanied by gibberish, like maybe he had some kind of mental disability. I took them to where they lived, a motel in the seedy motel neighborhood of south Modesto.

As I was heading for my next pickup, I recalled my original encounter with Rita a few days earlier on the way to Stockton. As far as I could tell, my attempt to explain that she was loved by God had no impact on her at all. Maybe I came across as a "preacher" no matter how hard I tried to be a regular guy.

Put me behind a pulpit in a church full of people, and I could usually get results. But my success rate with "escorts" was, so far, about zero.

Then I remembered how she had introduced me to her husband. She could have simply identified me as an Uber driver, or she could have said, "This is Steve, and he wouldn't let me smoke in his car." But she introduced me as a "pastor."

I felt a lump forming in my throat. Maybe that was the best I could expect. Maybe that was a win. My effort to tell her about the love of Jesus had not resulted in a dramatic conversion, but perhaps our conversation had moved her a few inches toward God.

I have not seen them since our trip from DD's Discounts to their home, but to this day, every time I drive by the Apex Motel, I say a little prayer for Rita and her family.

Déjà Vu All Over Again

I thought she was a nurse. I can't remember now what she had said that planted the seed in my mind, but I thought I was taking a nurse to work in a neighboring town. The ride had been requested by someone named Dale, which was not all that unusual. People regularly arranged a ride for a friend or family member.

I asked her where she worked, thinking it would be one of the hospitals in Stockton—St. Joseph's or Dameron. Instead, I was taking her to a place called the Déjà vu Club, which, as it turned out, was not a clinic for people who have the vague sense they have had an experience previously . . . but a strip club!

I asked her what she did there. I know, but at the time it seemed like a reasonable question. She could have been the bookkeeper or a waitress. She was an exotic dancer.

For a full five minutes, I was completely at a loss for what to say. What is the appropriate follow-up question to that admission? I was an ordained minister, giving a stripper a ride to work. I thought to myself, *I will need to tell Barb about this as soon as I get home.*

The next night, I got another ride request from Dale. He was at the mall and headed for a downtown hotel where he was staying. He started in with the normal questions: "How long have you been an Uber driver?"

"I have been driving Uber for about a year," I told him.
"How many days a week do you drive?"
"At least six days a week, and sometimes seven."
"Would you be willing to drive me and my friend, Jaelynn"—who I had met the night before—"to Stockton a few times a week?"

I realized his questions were sort of an interview, and I guess I got the job, because for the next several months, I was their standing ride to the Déjà Vu Club.

I would get a text with a time to be in Jaelynn's neighborhood, and then right on schedule, the ride request would pop up. I would pick her up, and then most of the time we would go get Dale and head for Stockton.

Over the course of those several months, I learned quite a lot about Jaelynn and Dale and the Déjà Vu.

Jaelynn was the mother of two small children and lived with "their father," as she put it. She was, of course, pretty—in a wholesome kind of way. If I had met her on the street or in the grocery store, I'd have never imagined she did what she did. I wasn't expecting her to dress provocatively or to wear glitter makeup all the time, but little about her matched what expectations I did have.

Dale was apparently a man of means. He talked about places where he had worked, but as far as I could tell, he didn't currently work at any of them. He just stayed at nice hotels and bought Jaelynn and her kids gifts and paid me to drive her to work.

I'm a naturally curious person. So while I wouldn't venture beyond the club's parking lot, I did work up the courage to ask a few questions over the course of my time as a Déjà Vu staff delivery driver.

One rule of the club was that a dancer cannot be accompanied by a "date" while working. That meant that I would drop off Dale at a bowling alley next door, where he would get a sandwich, and then he would go to the club, posing as a normal customer.

Another rule was that dancers must work at least six hours at a time. I had no idea why that was, but I still found it interesting.

Equally fascinating was the fact that Jaelynn had to pay the Déjà Vu Club for the time she was on stage, and then hope that the tips she got from customers would cover her expenses, plus leave some profit. I suppose that made her dancing an act of "commission." (A little joke for my Roman Catholic friends.)

It seemed to me that exotic dancers might benefit from some sort of union representation.

Once in a while, Jaelynn traveled to Stockton without Dale. We would chat for a while, and then about ten minutes into the trip, she would fall asleep for the remainder of the ride. It was completely understandable—a baby, a kindergartner, and a job that kept her awake until 3:00 a.m. two or three nights a week. I would grab a nap too. She would wake up as we pulled into the parking lot, and she would always apologize for falling asleep. I tried to assure her that it was fine and that the nap would do her some good.

As far as the nature of Dale and Jaelynn's relationship, I was stumped. Sometimes it seemed like they were just friends. He talked about other women that he was seeing, and she would give him relationship advice.

On other trips he would bring her gifts—flowers and teddy bears and that sort of thing—and compliment her on the way she looked. I thought for a while he might be a co-owner of the Déjà Vu and he was her sponsor, but that seemed unlikely, since he had to sneak in from the bowling alley an hour after her shift started.

What I really needed was one of those privacy screens with an electric window, like limousines have. They could have rolled up the window, and I would have just minded my own business. But a privacy screen was not even an available option when we bought our '05 Toyota Camry, and I assumed an aftermarket privacy screen would have been cost prohibitive.

Then all of a sudden . . . inexplicably . . . the rides stopped. No more trips to the Déjà Vu Club—nothing! I thought maybe I had done something wrong, or I figured that Dale, who certainly seemed well enough off to afford a car, had finally gotten one and replaced me.

But the story would end in a way that I could never have made up. About a month after I lost contact with the pair, I got a text message from Dale, asking me to call: "Could you give Jaelynn and me one last ride, Steve?"

"When were you thinking?" I asked.

"Could you meet us in downtown Modesto in thirty minutes?"

I was not in Uber mode for the day yet, but I told him I could swing forty-five minutes, and he said, "That would be fine."

When I pulled up to the DoubleTree Hotel, I was greeted with a bellhop cart completely loaded with suitcases, diapers, boxes, toys, and a stroller. There were four passengers, not two. I would also be giving a ride to Jaelynn's children. I said hello to everyone and told them how good it was to see them again. Jaelynn got the kids settled into the back seat while Dale and I packed and repacked two or three times before we got everything in the trunk.

Dale asked if we could stop at McDonald's on the way out of town. I suggested getting out of the downtown area, since the McDonald's on Modesto's 9th Street is, in my opinion, terrifying! He agreed, and so the five of us headed out.

We pulled into a McDonald's about twenty minutes later, and I asked if they wanted to go inside or use the drive-through. They opted for going inside, so I parked the car. Dale asked me if I wanted anything, and I said, "A medium Coke would be nice." Then, before I even knew what was happening, both Dale and Jaelynn got out of the car, leaving me with her kids!

There was total silence in the car until Jaelynn's little girl weakly uttered, "Mommy."

So I turned around in my seat and in my best reassuring voice said, "Your mommy will be right back. What's your name?" Her lower lip began to quiver. I offered to go first and said my name was Steve. I noticed an almost imperceptible change. She had just the slightest little grin on her face as she said, "Do you mean like the Steve in *Minecraft*?"

I knew exactly nothing about *Minecraft*, other than that it was some kind of video game, but I latched on to the connection. "Yes, just like in *Minecraft*."

She was using a kid's video tablet, so I asked what she was watching. It was an episode of *My Little Pony*, which I knew even less about than *Minecraft* (we had boys), but she proceeded to tell me about what the brands on each pony meant and who was good and which pony was bad and what their magic powers were. By the time the food arrived, I was a *My Little Pony* expert.

We headed out on the freeway again, and the food was distributed. The baby slept while they ate their burgers and Happy Meal. Pretty soon, things got quiet, and a glance toward the back seat confirmed that the kids and Jaelynn were asleep.

We drove on in silence for a few miles before Dale spoke up. He wanted to tell me what had been going on over the past few months. I should have said that he didn't owe me any explanation, but I was incredibly curious, so I listened.

"Working at the Déjà Vu Club was a very dark period for Jaelynn," Dale explained. "She didn't want to do it, but she believed it was what she had to do to help ensure the well-being of her family."

"We chose you as our regular driver because, for one thing, you had not hit on her, which was a problem with other drivers. And we picked you because you seemed kind . . . and didn't ask too many questions or get all judgy about what she did."

He explained that the "father of Jaelynn's kids" was not a nice guy and that she had filed for full custody of the girls. A hearing had been held, which the father didn't show up for, and so she was granted sole custody. And he told me that he had asked Jaelynn to marry him—and that she had said "yes." They were moving out of the Modesto area because there were just too many bad memories. And then he did something that I never, ever expected. He thanked me for being their friend.

It was so much more than I had bargained for. *Friend?* Here I thought I was just their Uber driver, making pretty good money running them to Stockton for a few months. But there were layers of complexity to the story that I had missed completely.

We arrived at their destination, another nice downtown hotel, and Dale got the bellhop cart and we loaded it up.

We stood at the trunk of my car. I finally said, "Well, I guess this is goodbye. It was nice to get to know you both, and your girls, Jaelynn."

Her eyes got misty. "Thank you."

Dale shook my hand and they left.

On the drive home, I thought about how things had worked out. Was it a fairytale ending? Not quite. Will they live happily ever after? I have no idea. But a young woman was rescued from a demeaning job and bad relationship. That counts for something.

And as for my small part, looking back, I had chosen to be kind. And in the end, that had counted for something too.

Kindness is getting harder and harder to come by these days. We drive without kindness. We express our opinions, often lacking basic kindness. We encounter people every day who could use a little kindness. So I have resolved to be nicer. Not to be a pushover or a doormat, but just to work toward kindness as my instinctive response.

I will never forget that there is an ex-stripper and her family out there who needed kindness—maybe more than anything else.

The Answer to Someone's Prayers

I figured it must have been ladies' night out when the three women came out of the restaurant and wine cafe called Camp 4 and climbed into the back of my car. They were having a good time laughing and joking with each other. Once they were all on board, I hit the Start Trip button and saw that our destination was another restaurant in Turlock. "Are you having a progressive dinner?" I inquired.

One of the ladies said, "I don't know what that is, but it sounds like fun."

"It means that a group travels from one house or restaurant to the next and they eat one part of a meal at every stop," I explained. "Appetizers at the first stop, salad at the next." I assumed they got the idea. They agreed that a progressive dinner sounded like fun, but that was not what they were doing.

One of the ladies explained that they were meeting their husbands at the pub where we were headed to eat dinner. The guys had been hanging out there while the ladies had been in Modesto.

As we were pulling out onto the street I said, "So this is a ladies' night out, guys' night out, progressive dinner, triple date?" They laughed and then started peppering me with questions.

"Is driving for Uber your full-time job?" one of the ladies asked.

"Yes it is, or at least I treat it like it is. I try to be out driving around forty hours a week, mostly from late afternoon until midnight. I guess that makes me the swing shift."

"What is the weirdest thing you have experienced as an Uber driver?"

"That's a tough one," I said, "because so many weird things happen."

They thought that was hilarious.

"What if I told you the most recent weird thing that happened?" I asked.

They agreed to my solution.

I told them about getting a ride request in east Modesto on the previous Friday night. When I found the address, I started waiting for someone to come out of the house, but after three or four minutes, there was no sign of life.

Some movement caught my eye in the rearview mirror, and I saw a woman in a white, full-length gown and elbow-length white gloves. She was peeking around a tree.

I got out of my car and asked if she had called an Uber. She turned out to be a he, and when I asked why he was hiding from me, he said, "I didn't know who you were and I was afraid."

I shot back, "Well that makes two of us. And that's a beautiful gown, by the way." My compliment must have allayed his fears. I opened the back door for him, and he got in.

I dropped him off at a downtown Modesto nightclub, where he might be considered slightly underdressed in his gown.

They wanted to know the longest trip I had taken and if I ever felt unsafe giving rides to complete strangers. They were full of questions and seemed to enjoy the stories I was telling them.

Eventually, one of the ladies asked what I did before driving for Uber. I thought, *Here we go. When I tell them I was a pastor for nearly all of my adult life, that will be the end of our conversation.* But I had never hesitated to tell the truth when someone asked that question, so I told them about my years in the church and how problems with my voice had forced a change of vocation.

It got quiet in the back seat, and I was sure that my confession of being an ordained minister turned Uber driver had brought our lively conversation to a screeching halt.

Finally, in hushed tones, one of the ladies said, "This is so cool."

I looked in the mirror and asked, "What is so cool?"

She told me that earlier in the evening, before a light meal that they had eaten together, they had prayed, and one of the things they had asked God for was an opportunity to be an encouragement to someone. Maybe a waiter or waitress or some stranger they would meet during the course of the evening. She said, "You are the one we prayed for."

We were arriving at their destination, and I was not quite sure how to respond. I have prayed for lots of people, but I had very little experience being the answer to someone's prayer.

I pulled into the parking lot of the restaurant and stopped, and one of the ladies asked if they could pray for me. I said, "Of course," and all three of them prayed the most wonderful, encouraging, affirming prayers that I had heard in a long time. When they were finished, I was humbled and overwhelmed with emotion. All I could say was "Thank you."

Since that experience, I have made an effort to be the answer to someone's prayers, at least once in a while. It's an effort because it requires admitting that you need some help or that you are struggling. It requires transparency and honesty, which, at least for me, are hard things to muster up.

Being the answer to someone's prayers also requires the effort of leaving some room in your prayers for what God wants to do with you.

My prayer list is mostly just that—a list of what I need God to be working on. My needs, my friend's stuff, my family concerns. What if we prayed every day that God would use us in a way that was strictly by His design? We might find ourselves in some wonderfully awkward and beautiful situations of which God was the sole architect.

CHAPTER 5

Final Impressions

T HE FOLLOWING STORIES DID NOT quite fit into the overall theme of *1000 Strangers In My Car*, but rather than leave them out in the cold, I have given them their own special place here in the back of the book. My passengers and I didn't always have big, memorable impacts on each other, but the encounters left an impression. I still wonder what became of many of the people I met and even remember some in my prayers.

A Glimpse into the Future

The argument was already underway when the couple got into my car. The man sat up front with me, and she sat in the back seat, which is unusual, but not unheard of. They were arguing, somewhat heatedly, about how many days it would be until some future event took place.

As I listened (I didn't really want to listen, but it was a car) I pieced together that I had picked them up after their engagement party, and the argument that was now underway concerned how many days remained before the wedding.

They were both defending numbers that were not too far in the future, but were not that close to each other. I don't remember exactly, but their "days until the wedding" figures were different by twelve or fourteen days. Somebody was way off. She began to deconstruct his arithmetic, and he just got louder. Things were getting out of hand.

Without any warning, the groom-to-be swung his attention in my direction and began to explain his formula for arriving at his number. It was complicated, but I think I was following him until he asked me to agree with his conclusion. I may not look very smart, but I am not so stupid as to intentionally inject myself into someone else's conflict. Agreeing with either one of them would be like slamming my own fingers in a car door. So I tried another tack: the evasive question.

"So where did you two meet?" I asked.

Amazingly, it seemed to work. There was a slight pause, and then she said, "We met in college. We have a mutual friend who was in my sorority, and she introduced us."

She went on to explain that they had been friends first, dated for about a year, were recently engaged, and were scheduled to be married in somewhere between ninety and one hundred and four days.

I thought the crisis had been averted, but then he asked me if I was married.

I said, "Yes, since 1982 . . . to the same woman!"

That earned me a slap on the shoulder and a few congratulatory remarks. Then came his follow-up question—"What's your secret?"

I knew what he was looking for: "three easy steps" or "five golden rules" that would guarantee success.

I decided to tell him what I told all the couples whose weddings I had officiated over the years. "The secret to a long and happy marriage is . . ." He leaned toward me in anticipation. I could sense his intense interest in "The Secret." I continued, "The secret is . . . there is no secret."

I explained that marriage is like anything else worthwhile and important. It takes effort and attention, and it takes work!

He stuck his head between the seats and said, "Babe, the Uber driver says that you are going to be high maintenance."

That was not what I meant, or said, so I tried a metaphor. "Marriage is like a flower garden. You can plant posies and marigolds, and they will come up and grow, but so will some weeds." I explained that the garden would need watering and fertilizing, and the weeds would need pulling.

He stuck his head into the back seat again and said, "The Uber Guy says you're a weed that needs pulling."

She shot back a few choice expletives and told him what he could do with his weeds.

And then he did something that made me want to open the door and push him out of my moving vehicle. He looked at me and rolled his eyes. Not a subtle, microsecond roll, but a full, melodramatic roll of the eyes. These two were in trouble.

They went back to arguing about the number of days until the wedding, and I just drove. And my mind went back to when I was performing weddings and the requirement I had that a couple meet with me for some basic premarital education sessions.

It was not heavy material. I'm not a counselor, but I would have them read a book called *Saving Your Marriage Before it Starts* by Drs. Lee and Leslie Parrott (Zondervan, 1995), and we would meet together and watch a DVD and discuss a chapter in each meeting. It's good, basic stuff: how to deal with unrealistic expectations, how to handle money, how to have a fair fight, that kind of thing.

In one chapter, the authors cited a study by Dr. John Gottman at the University of Washington. His claim was that he could predict, with around 87 percent accuracy, whether a couple would be married or divorced after seven years simply by watching how they handled each other in conflict.

If the couple practiced active listening and were kind and loving as they processed problems, their odds of remaining married were quite good. But if they were harsh and sarcastic and mean-spirited and "practiced disdain for each other, such as eye-rolling," they stood a much higher risk of divorce.

My passengers were still arguing about the date of their wedding when I dropped them off at their location. What they needed was a good calendar and maybe a calculator, or they might end up arguing about how many days until their divorce became final.

As I pulled out of the driveway onto the road back toward Modesto, I suddenly felt the weight of my self-righteous attitude pushing down on my chest, making it difficult to draw a full breath. I had been so busy predicting the inevitable failure of my engaged passengers marriage, I forgot to be grateful for the wife and the marriage that God had blessed me with.

Barb and I had the rare privilege of growing up in homes where our parents were "lifers" when it came to marriage. They meant it when they said "Till death do us part." We had front-row seats to a demonstration of how marriage should be done. Our parents were not perfect, but I can guarantee that there was very little "eye-rolling" that went on.

My predictions of failure and trouble for my recently delivered passengers turned into a prayer that somehow they would get past the "weeds" and enjoy the flowers they were planting together.

Ew!

I haven't watched *The Tonight Show with Jimmy Fallon*, but I am aware of an ongoing sketch on the show called "EW!" It's pronounced e-you, as in, "Ew, that's so gross."

Jimmy dresses up as a teenage girl named Sara (no *H*, because *H* is so . . . EW!) and, along with his guest stars, satirizes the tendency of the teen girl demographic to brutally observe the world they live in.

The whole premise of the ongoing "Ew!" sketch is that trashing everybody and everything around you is fun. It's like a sport, but instead of a soccer ball, you kick people all over the field. And everything and everybody is fair game—the way people look, dress, act, and talk. Nothing is off-limits.

I picked up two girls from the ritzy neighborhood near the Del Rio Country Club who were Ubering to a party together. They might have been the girls Jimmy Fallon based his "Ew!" characters on. They used the same slang and the same expressions ("seriously . . . Ew!").

It was like *The Tonight Show* in the back seat of my car. And they were clearly having a great time. They got out their smartphones and opened up Facebook or Instagram or Snapchat or whatevs (sorry) and proceeded to verbally annihilate everyone and everything they saw.

"Look at the guy Megan took to prom. His ears are so gross. They look like dinner plates."

"Seriously. I think there is an operation you can get to fix that. An ear tuck, or whatever."

"Ew! Someone should tell Marshall about Proactiv. His face is, like, gross."

I was wishing again for one of those limousine partitions with an electric window that I could just roll up and drive in silence. But it was a long trip—about thirty minutes—and I heard every word.

As I listened to the slander being volleyed around in the back seat, I recalled some of the situations where I had been impacted by gossip. I knew that, as a pastor, I had been the subject of plenty of conversations that centered around my leadership style or the content of my sermons. I stepped into the ministry understanding that this was part of the deal.

And to my shame, I thought about several situations where I had been a part of the problem. I had joined in with other leaders and complained about our church members in the name of catharsis. I had gossiped and called it "sharing" on more than one occasion. I had lost control of my tongue more times than I would like to admit.

What I hoped the young ladies in the back seat of my car would figure out is that gossip creates a kind of unwritten contract between the participants. It was an agreement that I had entered into many times.

What the gossip girls in the back seat were saying to each other was that by spending thirty minutes trashing their friends on Facebook they were essentially giving each other permission to do the same thing, except with another person.

You are writing each other a note that says, "I give you permission to assassinate my character. It may be on another Uber ride, or at a party, or over coffee . . . but feel free to kick me verbally in the head—hard!" That's what I wanted to say through the sliding glass partition that I didn't have in my 2005 Camry. "If she will gossip *with* you, she will gossip *about* you." *Ew.*

Church Hopping and Shopping

One of the experiments I conducted while Ubering was to see if driving on weekday mornings was any better, or at the very least, any worse, than Ubering at night. It was not unusual to go out on a weekday evening and Uber for eight hours and only make forty or fifty dollars. When you pay for your own gas and do the math, you realize you are making about four dollars an hour and that you would be better off rummaging through trash bins looking for soda cans.

On one of those experimental weekday mornings, I got a ride request from someone in Waterford, a little community about eight or ten miles east of Modesto. The great thing about a request from someone in Waterford is that they almost always want to go somewhere outside of Waterford, because Waterford is not exactly a tourist destination. (Sorry, citizens of Waterford.)

Sure enough, my passenger, a thirtysomething lady, needed a ride to her home in Stockton—about a sixty-mile trip. She had been visiting her boyfriend and his kids in Waterford. She got in and it became quickly apparent that she was interested in talking.

"Thanks for coming all the way out here to pick me up. Sometimes there are no Ubers available in the morning."

"No problem," I said. "I'm actually doing an experiment to see if driving on weekday mornings is any better or worse than driving at night."

"What's the verdict?" she asked.

"You're my first ride of the day, so things are going grrrreat!" I replied, doing my best Tony the Tiger impersonation.

She asked a few other general questions, and then the inevitable subject came up. She asked, "Is this your full-time job, or do you do something else?"

We were at the point when the conversation would either continue naturally or shrivel up and die. "My background is in the ministry, and I was a pastor for about thirty-five years," I said. "I started having some health problems, so for now, I'm a full-time Uber driver."

My confession didn't seem to bother her at all. In fact, she took the ball and ran with it. "Oh, I'm sorry to hear about your voice. That must be hard."

She went on to tell me that she had grown up in Stockton and had a background in the church as well.

"When I was in high school," she said, "like so many other teenagers, I drifted away from my church and did my own thing. I was pretty wild, and I got into some trouble."

She didn't go into any detail, but I assumed she had sewn some of the proverbial "wild oats." She told me about getting married and having several kids and then a divorce. Somewhere along the way, she had returned to her roots in the church and was now a believer.

The interesting thing about her story was that as she told it, she mentioned at least four or five congregations where she and her family had been a part of the fellowship, but then something went wrong and they moved on.

At one church, the pastor preached too many sermons on money. At another, the music was not their style. Or was it that the people were not friendly enough? I was having trouble keeping it all straight. We even drove by a church as we approached her home and she said, "I went there for a few years."

I asked what happened, and she described a feud that erupted over how a discipline problem with one of her kids had been handled. She got upset and left. I asked where she was attending currently, and she said, "Nowhere," but she was shopping for a new place to call home."

When I was pastoring in the local church, I used to get excited when a new couple or family or person would show up and, after the service, would say how much they loved my preaching or the music or the friendly people and how much better our church was than the place where they had pulled up stakes. But it didn't take long to learn that eventually (sometimes remarkably soon) I would step on their toes in a sermon, or our drums were too loud, or any of a number of perceived incompatibilities. And then I would get the inevitable phone call or visit at my office where they would let me know that they were moving on.

I was talking to a ministry colleague once about people jumping around from church to church.

He expressed his view: "It's just the normal ebb and flow of people moving from your church to another church."

My response was risky: "I usually feel like I just got dumped by my girlfriend when people leave. I take it personally. It usually hurts."

He looked at me with pity. "People leave. That's just the way it is."

Of course, there are valid reasons to leave a church: false teaching, abusive leadership, or blatant sin being tolerated. But in my humble opinion, most decisions to leave a church to go "shopping" are over issues that should, or at least could be, worked through and resolved to the betterment of the individuals involved and the church as a whole.

Maybe it was the realization that I would probably never see her again, or my experience in the church with people who "shop" for churches like they shop for furniture, but I decided to do a little truth-telling. In the few minutes we had left before I dropped her off, I challenged her to find a good church—one where the preaching was biblical and the leadership was godly. A church that had a well- defined mission where she and her family could be ministered to and do ministry. And then I told her that when things go wrong—because things always go wrong—she should stick it out and work through the conflict instead of packing up the kids and finding a new church home. The rest of the trip was pretty quiet.

Here is the bottom line: The only thing perfect about the church is her head (Jesus), and among the few sure things are problems. The church is populated by people, and people are dysfunctional and opinionated and broken and sinful. So you have a choice to make when (not if) the problems arise: work toward a solution and be refined by the process . . . or go shopping.

EPILOGUE

THE LATE CHRISTIAN FINANCIAL ADVISOR Larry Burkett said regarding his philosophy on the timing of replacing cars, "I drive a car till it turns to dust, then I sweep up the dust and ride on the dust."

My 2005 Toyota Camry turned over 260,000 miles while I was driving for Uber. That's more than enough to get to the moon, if you could drive there (average distance 238,900). It would take you around the world at the equator about 10.5 times if there were a road that followed the equator. And I used around 10,800 gallons of gas to go that far (combined city and highway average of 24 mpg).

The car has been a trooper since I drove it off the lot, especially as I used it for Ubering. Those miles really piled on quickly and took a heavy toll, as they tended to be mostly stop-and-go city driving.

Nothing major like the engine or the transmission failed or fell out while I was Ubering, but several peripheral systems did give out along the way. The water pump started leaking and making crunchy noises and had to be replaced. The alternator quit . . . alternating . . . and had to be changed out. And the starter failed in the parking lot of the Alexander Cohen Hospice House in Hughson, California, which I felt was quite fitting. Before any long Uber trip, I would say a prayer of blessing and, for good measure, invoke the spirit of St. Frances of Rome, the patron saint of automobiles.

At the same time, it seemed like my life was running parallel to the Camry's situation. My health stuff. The weakness of my voice, which forced me out of the pulpit. My mostly failed attempt to get a steady job. A dramatic hit in the income department. Nothing major was falling off, but my situation caused me to ask God what I believe to be a fair question: "What is going on here?"

But then I was reminded that the car analogy only works to a point. The comparison breaks down when you consider that we are God's most precious creation. We are His crowning achievement. People were created by God to be the object of His affection. People have eternal souls that God, motivated by love, sent His only Son to redeem. And cars are just, well, cars.

So God's plan is not to ride me into the ground like a pile of dust. Instead, He is continuing the process of making me into what He wants me to become. There may be some painful dismantling, some uncomfortable change, some restoration and reworking, but God is good and will continue to work on me if I am willing to let him.

***

Each time an Uber driver ends a ride, the rider is given the opportunity to give the driver a score using the one-to-five-star format. The driver is rated on their punctuality, their friendliness, the cleanliness of the car, etc., and if your average score gets too low, Uber can suspend your driving privileges.

But what most people don't know is that at the same time, the driver rates the rider with one to five stars as well. I would almost universally give a rider five stars, unless they were particularly obnoxious. One time, a guy ate his fast food dinner in the back seat and left greasy hamburger wrappers and open ketchup packets all over the place. I felt obligated to give him three stars. I found that almost every rider had a five star, or occasionally a four star, rating. I figured to get less than that would require the rider to regularly throw up in the back seat or be a serial killer.

My mom used to say, "Grow where you are planted." That's what I tried to do for my season as an Uber driver. I tried to see it as my ministry, and looking back, there were plenty of ministry opportunities.

But reality set in at tax time after a year of full-time Uber driving, when we crunched all the numbers. After subtracting the expenses of operating my own vehicle and paying all the taxes, I would have been way ahead working at the local Taco Bell for minimum wage!

I had to find more conventional work, so I redoubled my efforts and landed a part-time position at a very large company in our area working as a security guard. The job has developed into a full-time position with benefits and a pretty good hourly wage.

I am happy to report that I am still "growing where I am planted" and finding little bits of ministry every day. I am the first person employees and contractors see as they report to work, and I try to make sure they are welcomed warmly. I know most of their names, and we chat and laugh and show each other the latest pictures of our grandkids. I get in trouble regularly for slowing down traffic passing through my gate.

My head doesn't feel like it's going to explode very often any more, and I would like to thank the thousands of people I met while Ubering for helping me to find my voice.

It was a good ride—I give it five out of five stars.

Made in the USA
Monee, IL
10 January 2021